UTAH'S BIG FIVE NATIONAL PARKS

HARLEY AND ABBY MCALLISTER

MOUNTAINEERS BOOKS

 Mountaineers Books is the nonprofit publishing division of The Mountaineers, an organization founded in 1906 and dedicated to the exploration, preservation, and enjoyment of outdoor and wilderness areas.

1001 SW Klickitat Way, Suite 201 • Seattle, WA 98134
800.553.4453 • www.mountaineersbooks.org

Copyright © 2017 by Harley and Abby McAllister

All rights reserved. No part of this book may be reproduced or utilized in any form, or by any electronic, mechanical, or other means, without the prior written permission of the publisher.

Printed in China
Distributed in the United Kingdom by Cordee, www.cordee.co.uk
First edition, 2017

Copyeditor: Christy Karras
Design and layout: Heidi Smets
Cartographer: Lohnes+Wright
All photographs by the authors unless credited otherwise.
Page 6 caption: *Tunnel Arch is mesmerizing (Arches National Park)*
Cover photograph: *Collared lizard in Utah Canyonlands* (Stanislas_Verdonckt/iStock)

Library of Congress Cataloging-in-Publication data is on file for this title at https://lccn.loc.gov/2017028631

Mountaineers Books titles may be purchased for corporate, educational, or other promotional sales, and our authors are available for a wide range of events. For information on special discounts or booking an author, contact our customer service at 800-553-4453 or mbooks@mountaineersbooks.org.

ISBN (paperback): 978-1-68051-114-7
ISBN (ebook): 978-1-68051-115-4

CONTENTS

Introduction 9

How to Use This Book 11

5 Tips for Making the Most of Your Utah Vacation 12

Planning Your Utah Family Vacation 17

When to Go 17

Overview Map and Legend 18

Suggested Itineraries 20

Adding Adventure to Your Utah Trip 33

Best Bets 35

Arches National Park 35

Canyonlands National Park 37

Capitol Reef National Park 38

Bryce Canyon National Park 38

Zion National Park 41

Rafting in Southern Utah 42

Arches National Park 45

Getting to Arches 49

Arches Hiking Trips 49

Other Activities in Arches 66

Arches Camping and Lodging 68

Canyonlands National Park 71

Getting to Canyonlands 72

Island in the Sky Hiking Trips 74

Other Activities in Canyonlands 82

Canyonlands Camping and Lodging 85

Capitol Reef National Park 87

Getting to Capitol Reef 89

Capitol Reef Hiking Trips 90

Other Activities in Capitol Reef 106

Capitol Reef Camping and Lodging 107

Bryce Canyon National Park 111

Getting to Bryce Canyon 115

Bryce Canyon Hiking Trips 117

Other Activities in Bryce Canyon 131

Bryce Canyon Camping and Lodging 133

Zion National Park 137

Getting to Zion 141

Zion Hiking Trips 143

Inside Zion Canyon
(Shuttle Route) 143

Other Trip Options in
Zion Canyon 153

Outside Zion Canyon 154

Other Activities in Zion 160

Zion Camping and Lodging 163

Day Trip: Grand Canyon National Park–North Rim 164

Safety in the Parks 171

Temperature 171

Dehydration 173

Flash Floods 174

Snakebites 176

First-Aid Kits 176

Travel Checklists 178

Wildlife Spotting Checklists 178

First-Aid Kit Checklist 180

Day Hiking Checklist 181

Resources 182

Index 186

A feeling of accomplishment!

INTRODUCTION

Where can you find immense rock faces, deep canyon gorges, arches spanning the sky, nights dark enough to see a million stars, mysterious remains of ancient peoples, and slot canyons so narrow you must side-shimmy to get through? We found all of this and more in Utah's national parks. Our kids thought we had entered an enchanted land as we moved from one park to the next on our first visit to some of the most distinctive places we have ever seen. Although most of these parks are relatively close to each other on the map, each has its own unique character and geology. Our kids became explorers, adventurers, leaders, team members, climbers, daredevils, and renegades as they discovered each new park and all it offered.

Would you love to explore one or more of these parks? What would it be like to see your child come alive with wonder and a desire to run ahead of you and make their own discoveries? We want to help you plan a vacation that will ignite passion and enthusiasm in your kids—and help you enjoy your vacation more. Read on to find suggestions tailored to traveling and exploring with kids, hiking ideas in each park written with your kids in mind, must-see attractions for those on a tighter timeline, suggested itineraries, and more.

According to our boys, the rockier the better (Zion National Park)

HOW TO USE THIS BOOK

Most people planning to visit one Utah park will choose to explore at least one other park, since they are in close proximity to one another. When we were first planning a trip to southern Utah, it was difficult for us to know how much time to spend in each park and how to spend our time once we were there. In thinking through how to best share all we learned, we realized that choosing an overall itinerary and then filling it in with specific hikes and adventures would be most helpful. To that end, we have included a section of suggested itineraries before we detail all of the adventures we recommend for each park. Look through that section with your allotted vacation time in mind and find a schedule that fits your family. After choosing your itinerary, reading the sections about the parks you plan to visit will allow you to plan each day. We hope this will streamline your planning time and give you confidence that you'll be able to do all you want to on this amazing vacation!

For each park, you will find detailed information to help you choose the best hikes and other adventures for your particular family. The hikes are listed by name, followed by a brief description. Additionally, you will find directions to get you to the trailhead or starting point, and approximate distances and an estimated time needed to complete the hike. We include directions for any turns off the main trails, obstacles, or items of special interest along the way. And we give suggestions for good places to rest, snack, and even picnic! Some of these details are a little subjective. The times listed are based on our own experiences with our active children, aged eight to twelve (plus a baby in a backpack!), and don't include the time spent playing once we reached the main attraction. Distances are usually roundtrip

Stops with views like this keep even the drives in Utah's Big 5 National Parks amazing.

for out-and-back hikes, and we indicate which are loops; there are a few exceptions when we recommend going one-way only. We consider several hundred feet of elevation gain per mile to be moderate; less than that is easy and more would count as difficult. In reality, rather than hard and fast rules and numbers, we have based our descriptions on how we felt when we were actually hiking the trail. Our times tend to be toward the shorter end of the spectrum because our kids have abundant energy, so use the numbers as guidelines and choose the best hikes to match your own kids' levels of energy and interest.

5 TIPS FOR MAKING THE MOST OF YOUR UTAH VACATION

1. Bring a lot of water.

You will need more water than you might normally need to function. Heed the warning signs and bring plenty. Often our children don't think to drink when they're scampering all over rocks, so we make a point of stopping them and making them drink. We designate one water bottle with an easily measureable volume for each person so we can see how much each child is consuming daily. Even if you're not showing signs of sweating, remember that the arid environment around you is stealing water right off your skin. Since you're losing water, you need to make sure to replenish regularly throughout the day.

2. Learn to navigate in a desert environment.

Deserts can be harsh yet beautiful places to explore. For many people, conditions they find in the desert are new and alien. Even for veteran outdoorsmen and women, desert exploration often presents a new set of conditions to appreciate and techniques to acquire. There are things we can all learn, especially in the areas of navigating and routefinding. In particular, you may notice something new along the trail that you haven't seen in other places: little stacks of rocks called cairns.

People charged with marking trails often find it difficult to place signs that will last in dry conditions without damaging the landscape. Arid environments are also often devoid of much vegetation, and posted signs would greatly impact the visual aesthetics. Rather than posting signs, people often make small piles of stones to mark the trail. Sometimes unknowing children will think it great sport to either knock down the piles or add more of their own along the way. This should be discouraged, as it makes routefinding difficult for those coming behind. As you're hiking, make sure you walk slowly, scanning the entire area. If you find yourself in a spot where the trail seems to disappear (on sandstone, for example), you will usually spot one of these cairns, confirming you are on the right trail. One of our suggested hikes in the more remote part of Capitol Reef National Park, Headquarters Canyon, requires careful observation at many points in order to locate cairns and find the correct trail.

3. Plan ahead.

When thinking about activities, be sure to take into account the hottest parts of the day and plan accordingly. There's nothing wrong with an enforced rest time during the middle of the day, and if you plan carefully, you can enjoy a shaded campsite while the sun is at its strongest. If you choose to hike, we recommend some that offer more shade; saving those for the hot time of day is wise. Midday is also a good time to explore visitor centers. In Arches National Park there's a nice interpretive walk-through display that's interactive for kids. The back of the visitor center is a tall glass window that allows you to view different aspects of the sandstone from inside. There is, of course, a park video too. Save these for the hot parts of the day instead of going first thing in the morning when you arrive or the last thing as you leave.

4. Take advantage of park programs.

Each park offers the Junior Ranger program that includes a free booklet, filled with age-appropriate activities children complete in order to attain the title of Junior Ranger. The activities teach kids how and why to protect the park environment. Once they complete it, they are sworn in by a real ranger to support

Being sworn in as a Junior Ranger is a point of pride for kids. (NPS photo)

and defend the park, and they are given a badge they can wear proudly. These activities are fun and educational, and they give kids something to do during inevitable time in the car or the hottest parts of the day when you're not out hiking. Our kids always have enjoyed this program in every park that offers it, and we're sure yours will too. These booklets can be picked up at any visitor center—and the best part is they're free!

Another free program offered by the parks is the Family Explorer pack. These are backpacks (or satchels) filled with books, a magnifying glass, binoculars, workbooks, and any other supplies necessary to complete the included activity sheets. These activities are designed to encourage observing the park using all the senses, which is perfect for kids. The directions in the pack say that you can do certain activities in lieu of the Junior Ranger activities but still receive the badge. When we tried to do that, none of the rangers believed us. We showed them the directions and they honored it but didn't like it, so clarify ahead of time what they will accept for a Junior Ranger badge. Overall our kids liked the Junior Ranger materials better, but it's worthwhile simply to use the parts your kids find interesting. You can check the bag out for seven days, and usually you can return it at one of the other nearby parks. Inquire for details at the visitor center.

One final "freebie" our whole family enjoys is the Passport to Your National Parks book. While the book isn't free (currently $10 each), once you own it, you can fill it with free stamps at any visitor center. The cancellation-type stamp includes the date and an image. There are also places to add stickers you can buy showcasing various regions, wildlife, and iconic scenes. If you want to avoid buying the book, help your kids create their own booklet at home. Anyone can use the stamp station whether they have purchased a book or not.

5. Explore—carefully.

Kids love to explore. For our boys, if it's on a main trail, it's intrinsically not as interesting as something off the beaten path. It's great to let your kids explore, but the desert environment is very fragile. Take the time to know when and where kids can be free to range and roam and when they need to be more contained. In many places you will encounter what are known as "social trails." These trails are not part of the official trail system but are created by people continually leaving the main trail to take a shortcut or to see some feature of interest. Unfortunately, these social trails damage sensitive areas, lead to erosion problems, and generally make areas less scenic. Do your best to keep your kids on the main trail to avoid adding to these problems. We involve our kids in understanding the when and why and remind them that places like these belong to all of us.

Programs like Junior Ranger do a great job of inviting kids into the role of caretaker. In particular, Arches has a large population of cryptobiotic-crust soil that is extremely important and equally fragile. Cryptobiotic crust is a colony of bacteria, algae, and lichens that bind thin desert soil together in clumps that are darker and slightly more prominent than the surrounding earth. These colonies protect the soil from erosion and dissipation by wind, but they are no match for a boot or shoe step. The organisms in these colonies take anywhere from 45 to 250 years to regrow. Teaching your kids to spot these colonies and avoid them will protect our desert ecosystems in a vital way.

PLANNING YOUR UTAH FAMILY VACATION

OVERVIEW MAP AND DRIVING DISTANCES

Our map of the Big 5 national parks gives you an idea of how they are related to each other geographically. A table of driving distances between the different parks follows the map.

What doesn't necessarily show in the map below is how close Las Vegas is to Zion—a mere 161 miles, or about two and a half hours by car. Since flights to Las Vegas are often cheap, this can be a great option if you're focusing on the western parks. But if you're going all the way to Moab it will be a long drive back to catch your flight home. Of course, you could use this time to go south on the way back and see Monument Valley and the North Rim of the Grand Canyon! This will be an important consideration when you're deciding your starting and ending locations.

WHEN TO GO

Understanding the climate and weather of Utah's desert parks is critical to planning a successful trip for your family. Many people erroneously believe that a desert is always a hot and therefore great place to visit at any time of year. Actually, the desert can be very cold at certain times and very inhospitable, especially to young children.

Arches, Canyonlands, and Capitol Reef National Parks

This part of Utah is on what is known as the Colorado Plateau and is a classic high desert characterized by wide temperature swings due to the elevation and the dry air. In fact, daily temperatures here can fluctuate by as much as forty degrees Fahrenheit, so you really need to come prepared for most anything. In late summer, monsoon moisture can come in a hurry in

Driving Distances between Parks (in miles)

	Arches	Bryce	Canyon-lands	Capitol Reef	Zion	Las Vegas	Salt Lake City
Arches		264	32	142	341	454	229
Bryce	264		282	116	85	250	270
Canyonlands	32	282		221	324	465	247
Capitol Reef	142	116	221		183	353	217
Zion	341	85	324	183		161	307
Las Vegas	454	250	465	353	161		421
Salt Lake City	229	270	247	217	307	421	

the form of thundercloud bursts that lead to local flooding, so always consider the forecast when planning excursions.

Bryce Canyon National Park

Although called a canyon, this park has the highest elevations of all the Utah parks because the main visitor areas are situated atop a high plateau. Its rim elevation varies from 8000 to 9000 feet at its southern end, so you might find yourself short of breath at times. You will definitely find yourself less warm here, as average temperatures are roughly ten degrees cooler than in the neighboring national parks. Average lows for this park are below freezing for eight months of the year, and even in the warmest months, the low temperatures will typically be in the forties. You will definitely want to bring warmer clothes and dress in layers when visiting Bryce.

Zion National Park

The valley floor of Zion National Park is at 4000 feet, and it has relatively mild winters and hot summers. However, due to the elevation and dry climate, day and night temperatures may differ by more than thirty degrees. On hot days it's best to plan your more strenuous activities for early and late in the day, when the steep canyon walls provide relief from the sun.

SUGGESTED ITINERARIES

Trying to determine how best to spend whatever time you have can be one of the most daunting and challenging aspects of planning a trip, particularly when you're traveling to a new area. Truly taking advantage of all this region has to offer could literally take a month, but who among us has that much time? Maybe in retirement, but probably not while we're raising families!

Temperatures and Precipitation in Utah's Big Five National Parks

Month	Average High (F°)	Average Low (F°)	Record High (F°)	Record Low (F°)	Average Precipitation
Arches and Canyonlands National Parks					
January	44	22	63	–1	0.6
February	52	28	73	9	0.63
March	64	35	87	13	0.77
April	71	42	93	25	0.79
May	82	51	105	33	0.76
June	93	60	110	43	0.47
July	100	67	116	51	0.68
August	97	66	109	44	0.81
September	88	55	105	36	0.89
October	74	42	106	23	1.15
November	56	30	79	12	0.57
December	45	23	69	5	0.44
Capitol Reef National Park					
January	41	20	64	–2	0.49
February	47	26	71	–7	0.55
March	58	33	80	11	0.52
April	66	40	88	22	0.57
May	75	48	97	29	0.61
June	87	58	103	35	0.34
July	91	65	104	51	1.01
August	88	63	101	50	1.21
September	80	54	96	35	0.95
October	66	44	88	23	0.87
November	51	31	74	11	0.53
December	41	21	67	–7	0.34

In order to help you make the most of your time, we suggest itineraries for stays of various lengths—three, five, and seven or more days. These itineraries are fairly generic by necessity, because yours will depend a great deal on what your starting point is, how much hiking you want to do, what lodging options you prefer, how much you're willing to drive, what your budget is, and how you're getting there. We can't anticipate answers

Temperatures and Precipitation in Utah's Big Five National Parks

Month	Average High (F°)	Average Low (F°)	Record High (F°)	Record Low (F°)	Average Precipitation
Bryce Canyon National Parks					
January	39	9	62	–30	1.7
February	41	13	66	–29	1.4
March	46	17	76	–13	1.4
April	56	25	82	–5	1.2
May	66	31	89	5	0.8
June	76	38	96	20	0.6
July	83	47	97	25	1.4
August	80	45	94	17	2.2
September	74	37	91	17	1.4
October	63	29	85	–2	1.4
November	51	19	75	–20	1.2
December	42	11	67	–23	1.6
Zion National Park					
January	52	29	71	–2	1.6
February	57	31	78	4	1.6
March	63	36	86	12	1.7
April	73	43	94	23	1.3
May	83	52	102	22	0.7
June	93	60	114	40	0.6
July	100	68	115	51	0.8
August	97	66	111	50	1.6
September	91	60	110	33	0.8
October	78	49	97	23	1.0
November	63	37	83	13	1.2
December	53	30	71	6	1.5

Hikers are dwarfed by the scale of the canyon in Zion National Park.

Fall is a beautiful time of year to visit Bryce Canyon National Park.

to all those questions, but we *can* provide enough details to create a framework you can then fill in based on your individual situation. So let's get started!

Three-Day Itineraries

If you have only three days to spend, you should not try to see all the parks. Instead, the best approach would be to divide the parks into western (Zion and Bryce) and eastern (Arches and Canyonlands) groups and decide which ones you most want to visit. Then, depending on which activities you choose, you could also fit in a day trip to Capitol Reef, which is roughly in the middle of the two groups.

Westside Parks
Day 1: Zion National Park

You will only have a day here, so focus your time in the heart of the park: Zion Canyon. Ride the shuttle and take advantage of the stops to select two or three of the hikes we've suggested, or perhaps a horseback ride. If you have time left, you could head to the tunnel near the east entrance and do the Canyon Overlook hike at sunset, when it's particularly magical.

Day 2: Bryce Canyon National Park or North Rim of the Grand Canyon

From the east entrance of Zion National Park, it's a mere two and a half hours to the North Rim of the Grand Canyon so it's a great opportunity to check this off your bucket list. Then, later that evening or on the following day, you could continue on to Bryce Canyon National Park, which is a three-and-a-half-hour drive. Just keep in mind that Arizona doesn't participate in Daylights Savings Time, so half the year they're an hour behind Utah time! If you go directly to Bryce from Zion, it's only a one-and-a-half-hour drive, and this will leave time to explore what Bryce Canyon has to offer. At a minimum, drive or take the shuttle to the most well-known overlooks; but if at all possible, do one of the suggested hiking routes that drops below the rim and gets you in among the hoodoos (the name given the strange-looking columnar formations).

Day 3: Capitol Reef National Park

If you went to the Grand Canyon on day 2, then day 3 should be spent at Bryce Canyon. However, if you went directly to Bryce Canyon on day 2, you should drive State Route 12 up to Capitol Reef National Park. This scenic byway is beautiful any time of year, but if you happen to catch it at the height of the fall aspen colors (early October) it will simply take your breath away.

Driving this route will also take you past Grand Staircase–Escalante National Monument, where you could easily spend another three days! Our website features several amazing slot canyon hikes not too far off SR 12 and a waterfall hike, to Lower Calf Creek Falls, that you will pass on your drive. Even the car time along this scenic route will be memorable.

Hiking in a hoodoo wonderland

Once you arrive in Capitol Reef, take the scenic drive that leaves south from the visitor center and be sure to leave enough time to sample the pies at the Gifford House. There are also several quick hikes near the main area that we've included that are well worth the effort.

Eastside Parks

If you're visiting the eastside parks, your base of operations will be Moab, Utah. From here it's a mere 5 miles to the Arches National Park entrance and only 32 to the Canyonlands Island in the Sky district. You'll have two days to see Arches and Canyonlands; you will want to devote more of this time to Arches. It has more to offer families and some great hikes, whereas Canyonlands has a few key spots you can drive to, with a few short hikes thrown in if you choose. Your third day could be spent visiting Capitol Reef National Park or perhaps taking a day to sample one of Moab's many adventures: river rafting, mountain biking, or four-wheel-drive (4x4) trails on Bureau of Land Management (BLM) land.

Day 1: Arches National Park

Get up early to see all that Arches National Park has to offer. The 36-mile scenic loop drive can take about two and a half hours, but to really experience the flavor of Arches, you'll want to get out of your car. Head to the Windows section for a couple short walks that display some awesome arches, then go all the way up north to do our favorite hike: Devils Garden and its many and varied arches.

Day 2: Arches and Canyonlands National Parks

Start the day in Arches to catch sunrise over Delicate Arch, perhaps the most iconic view in all of Utah. While there is a strenuous, 3-mile roundtrip hike (with 480 feet of elevation gain) that you can take to its base, you can also see it from afar at much more easily reached viewpoints. After this, make your way over to the Canyonlands National Park Island in the

Sky district. Here you will want to drive to Grand View Point and Green River Overlook for amazing vistas reminiscent of the Grand Canyon. The Green River Overlook is especially impressive at sunset. You'll probably also have time for the short hike to Mesa Arch, which is right off the main road; and if you have time beyond that, you should make your way over to Upheaval Dome, where another short hike brings you to the precipice of an amazing geologic wonder.

Day 3: Capitol Reef National Park or Moab Adventure

From Moab it's only two and a half hours to Capitol Reef National Park, which surprisingly is nothing like the two parks you just visited. Once you arrive in Capitol Reef, take Scenic Drive, which heads south from the visitor center, and sample the pies at the Gifford House. If you have time there are also several quick hikes near the main road that are well worth the effort.

Otherwise you could spend this day taking advantage of some of the adventurous activities that the Moab area has to offer. River rafting, mountain biking, or backcountry 4x4 driving tours are all on the menu if this sparks an interest.

For movie buffs, it's a two-and-a-half-hour drive from Moab to Monument Valley, on the border with Arizona. This was the backdrop for several of John Ford's classic westerns and is an impressive sight whether you recognize it from the silver screen or not.

Five-Day Itineraries

Five parks in five days—seems tempting, doesn't it? This plan is possible, but it might turn your trip into more of a road rally than a real outdoors vacation. And nothing bores children as much as spending countless hours in the car without the chance to step outside and experience things by touch, sight, and smell. We suggest that you resist the temptation to simply drive from one national park to the next, "bagging" one each day, as it wouldn't leave much time to actually appreciate what you're seeing or experience anything but the surface of what they have to offer. But it could be done. Simply start at one side of the state and at the end of each day drive to the next park. Visitor centers always have park newspapers that will tell you the main points to hit if you have just a day to visit.

On the other hand, five days will give you a pretty good amount of time to experience three parks of your choosing at a deeper level. Once again, we'd suggest dividing your options into the western or eastern parks and then spending a bit more time in each.

Westside Parks
Days 1 and 2: Zion National Park

You will want to spend most of your time in Zion Canyon, riding the shuttle to the various stops and choosing the hikes that sound the most interesting to you. You should also have time to participate in some of the ranger-led activities and still have half the day to explore one of the options in the eastern portion of the park. We review some hidden canyons there that are tons of fun to explore and the Canyon Overlook Trail which is well known for good reason.

Kids of all ages need to experience the outdoors!

Day 3: Grand Canyon National Park

From the east entrance of Zion it's only two and a half hours to the North Rim of the Grand Canyon, and that makes this a very doable day trip. The North Rim is higher in elevation than the south and offers beautiful aspen and pine forests to complement the red-rock canyon, so why not go and check this off your bucket list?

Day 4: Bryce Canyon National Park

You will want to overnight near this park so that you really get a full day here. You can drive to several wonderful viewpoints, but there are even better hikes that require moderate effort and take you right in among the hoodoos. This is also a good place to get in a horseback ride if you and the kids are inclined. Finally, the nighttime "Dark Ranger" programs here are another excellent reason to spend the night in or near Bryce Canyon.

Day 5: Highway 12 and Capitol Reef National Park

It may seem strange to mention a highway as an attraction, but State Route 12 (usually called Highway 12) is a scenic byway that goes through wonderful areas that are full of opportunity. You will drive right through Grand Staircase–Escalante National Monument, which offers a few amazing slot-canyon hikes all its own. Check out our website for more details.

The first part of this day could be spent going deeper into Bryce Canyon or experiencing some of the options along SR 12 in Grand Staircase or the towns along the way, but leave enough time to arrive in Capitol Reef National Park by midday. You will want to do the scenic drive that goes south from the visitor center into the park and check out the orchards and historic ranch buildings. There are several moderate hikes near the center of this park worth doing, and the sunset against the Waterpocket Fold is memorable.

Delicate Arch with a backdrop of the La Sal Mountains—where else but Arches National Park?

Eastside Parks
Days 1 and 2: Arches National Park

Arches National Park offers so much to see and so many hikes of various levels that you can easily spend two full days here and wish you had just a little more time. Mornings are cooler and therefore make good times for longer hikes like Devils Garden (our favorite) or those that are exposed to the sun, like Delicate Arch. Then, in the afternoon, you can go experience some of the other must-see locations in the Windows Section of the park, as well as Balanced Rock, Park Avenue, and the various drive-to pullouts and viewpoints.

Day 3: Canyonlands National Park

From Moab it's just a 32-mile drive to the Island in the Sky district of Canyonlands. This means that with an early start you can experience much of what this park has to offer in just one day. Mesa Arch is a quick, short hike off the main road and a great place to witness sunrise or the early morning hours. From there you can drive south to Grand View Point and join in a ranger-led hike that leaves from that area. Later in the day you should head to the northwest portion of the park to check out Upheaval Dome and some of the other moderate hikes in that area, but save sunset for the view from the Green River Overlook, the best spot to watch the sun go down.

P.S. On the drive between Arches and Canyonlands, there's a relatively short side road that leads to Dead Horse Point Overlook. This famous and fantastic view is in a state park of the same name, but don't spend too much time here or you may feel rushed in Canyonlands.

Day 4: Capitol Reef National Park

It's going to take a few hours to drive from the Moab area to Capitol Reef, but you will still have time and enjoy your stay there. Capitol Reef tends to have fewer and shorter hikes that are great for kids; select one from our list and make the most of it. Hickman Bridge is the most popular and is a good choice. If your kids have never seen petroglyphs, you should make time for that short boardwalk excursion. We also enjoyed Cohab Canyon for its diversity of experiences. No matter what hike you choose, be sure to leave some time to experience the pies at the Gifford House. This is also one park where the scenic drives really do give you some spectacular scenery from the comfort of your car. At the end of the day, a short drive to Panorama Point is a gorgeous way to watch the sun set.

Day 5: Other Adventures

Your fifth day could easily be spent experiencing more of what each of these parks has to offer, but it's also an opportunity to get out and do something unique to this area. The Moab region is famous for its rugged back roads running through endless stretches of surrounding BLM land. You can experience this from a mountain bike, an off-road vehicle, a 4x4, or even a dirt bike. The Moab visitor center website or a quick internet search for "Moab adventures" will turn up countless options, depending on what you're looking for.

Another great option that may seem surprising in this desert land is to go rafting. The water you'd be floating on does not come from the minimal rain in this area but begins far away in the Colorado and Wyoming Rockies. The Green and Colorado rivers join in Canyonlands National Park, and their currents have shaped this land. They can also shape your experience! You can have either a scenic float or a thrilling whitewater adventure just a short drive from Moab. Check out Rafting in Southern Utah in the Best Bets chapter for more specifics.

GRAND STAIRCASE-ESCALANTE NATIONAL MONUMENT

Grand Staircase–Escalante National Monument probably deserves a chapter all its own; it's just less developed than its national park neighbors. Because it's not a national park, we have not included a full review of it in this book. However, there are famous slot canyons here, like Spooky Gulch and Peek-a-Boo Gulch, that are delightful to explore, and it has a Devils Garden of its own. The hikes we took in Grand Staircase were some of the best we've ever done! If you're interested in famous true slot canyons, otherworldly rock formations, or hikes to incredible waterfalls, check out the trip reports on our website. If you do go, there's a great campground at Calf Creek Falls, right off Highway 12, that is also the starting point for a waterfall hike. It's difficult to get a spot here but well worth a try, as there are no other developed camping areas nearby. You are allowed to dry camp in any "disturbed area" in the monument, but we found this to be a very unpleasant experience. If you're willing to drive another half hour, you can also try for a site at Escalante Petrified Forest State Park north of the town of Escalante.

Seven Days and Beyond

If you're fortunate enough to have seven or more days dedicated to your family vacation, you're in for a real treat. With this much time, it's reasonable to try and hit each of the Big 5 parks and still feel like you really got to experience each one. The descriptions in our three- and five-day itineraries will help you decide what you want to do in each park; here we suggest how much time to devote to each park:

Arches National Park: 2 days
Canyonlands National Park: 1 day
Capitol Reef National Park: half a day
Bryce Canyon National Park: 1.5 days
Zion National Park: 2 days

ADDING ADVENTURE TO YOUR UTAH TRIP

As you add days beyond seven, your options expand rapidly. This is because you can always explore each national park more deeply, but there are also many things to do in surrounding areas. Here are some suggestions:

Near Arches and Canyonlands National Parks

MOUNTAIN BIKING: This area is famous for it, and you can rent anything you need in Moab.

RIDING 4X4S: There are countless miles of primitive and adventure-filled roads in surrounding BLM lands and plenty of guides and rental companies to help you explore them.

RAFTING: Cataract Canyon, nearby on the Colorado River, is good for river trips of anywhere from half a day to seven days. See Rafting in Southern Utah in the Best Bets chapter for more details.

SIGHTSEEING: In addition to the off-road and rafting adventures this area is known for, you could also drive 150 miles south to Monument Valley, the site of many famous westerns.

Near Capitol Reef and Bryce Canyon National Parks

EXPLORING HIGHWAY 12: This is the preferred route between these two parks, and it has much to offer. It goes from high mountains brimming with aspens and wildlife to desert lowlands that offer dramatic views as you navigate the twisty byways.

RIDING 4X4S: A number of back roads connect the more remote areas of Capitol Reef to some of the smaller neighboring towns. The most notable is the Burr Trail Road linking the remote southern portion of the park to the town of Boulder, which lies on Highway 12. It's mostly paved, but offshoots and other nearby roads are dirt.

Near Zion National Park

NORTH RIM OF THE GRAND CANYON: As you travel between the east entrance of Zion National Park and Bryce Canyon National Park, you'll be tempted to make a side trip to the North Rim of the Grand Canyon. It's only about two hours in each direction out of your way, so why not give in and go check it out? We did, and we have never regretted the day it added to our most recent trip. Remember that Arizona does not change clocks for daylight saving time, so your clocks may be off by an hour, depending on what time of year you go. This is especially important if you plan to attend a ranger-led hike or program!

CEDAR BREAKS NATIONAL MONUMENT: This is basically a smaller replica of Bryce Canyon with a little flavor of its own. It's a defunct volcano flow with plenty of interesting geology, an alpine crater lake, wildflower meadows, and waterfalls. And much of it is easily accessible from the road.

Now for the fun part! In the next chapter, you will find detailed activity options for each park. Read through them and choose the ones you think will best fit your group's interests and fitness levels.

BEST BETS

Whatever your personal preference in hikes and adventures, some sights just should not be missed. This chapter gives you an idea of hikes or drives you will want to include in your trip planning. We go into more detail on each suggestion in the park-specific chapters.

Arches National Park

There are so many amazing sights in Arches that it's hard to choose just a few! First, Delicate Arch is possibly the most iconic image in all of southern Utah (you will see it immortalized on state license plates!), so you will want to make your way out to see it. One option is the overlook reached via a short walk from the parking area. Or you can choose to lace up your boots and complete the strenuous hike for an up-close view—just don't try it midday in the summer. Either way, you won't want to miss this sight.

Balanced Rock has a parking area right off the main road, so this is an easy and memorable one to check off the list. From there you will want to drive east to the Windows Section, where a series of short walks takes you to the feet of some of the park's most impressive arches: Double Arch, the North and South Windows, and others.

If you're up for a longer and slightly more challenging hike, we recommend making your way to the Devils Garden trailhead. From here it's an easy walk to witness Landscape Arch, which is the widest arch you will see. After this point the trail gets much more challenging as it heads out to Double O Arch, but in a way that is really fun for older and more capable kids.

Who wants to explore?

It also showcases a few unusual arches on side hikes along the way. This was our family's favorite hike in Arches.

While either going to or coming from Devils Garden, don't miss the quick side hike to Sand Dune Arch. Although it's not the most impressive in terms of scale, it's very charming, and the canyon that contains it is shady and cool on a hot day, with a lot of little rocks and fins that kids can scramble on and explore and a nice sandy area for playing. It's the perfect place to let your kids burn off some of that energy pent up from a lot of driving.

Canyonlands National Park

One of the main attractions in this area is the view—really we should say the views, plural. As you approach the park from the north, you're already on a mesa, so you have no clue of what is to come. As you make your way into the park, you begin to see how the ground falls away sharply, providing you with stunning vistas. But it isn't until you're able to visit the numerous overlooks that you fully appreciate this region of the park. You'll want to make a point of visiting at least a few of the fantastic overlooks Canyonlands offers.

The most expansive view in the park is at Grand View Point, at the southern terminus of the park's road system. Check at the visitor center for ranger-led activities.

If you're in the park for sunset, you will certainly want to make your way to the Green River Overlook as well. The final rays of the sun dropping below the horizon light up the cliffs in a golden glow that is beautiful to behold.

The most popular hike in the park is Mesa Arch, and for good reason. It's a short hike to a beautiful view and very accessible from the main road. The arch itself may not seem dramatic if you've recently come from Arches National Park, but the views behind and beyond the arch make this one memorable, especially in the morning.

Now, most kids are not that hot on scenic vistas; one or two a trip is enough for them. It's usually more of an adult thing, but not so in Canyonlands! Each overlook here is paired with something new and unique that captures kids' attention and gives you a bit more time to soak up the scenery. Check out the hiking trips in the Canyonlands chapter to find views paired with arches, ruins, rock scrambling, stargazing, and more!

Capitol Reef National Park

In order to capture the flavor of Capitol Reef National Park, you should have three things on your must-see list. The Waterpocket Fold is the main geologic feature shaping this whole park so you must take the time to see it. Our favorite way to do this is via the scenic drive that leaves from the visitor center and goes south along the western edge of the fold. We usually don't recommend driving much with your kids, but this drive is worth it, for you at least. You may want to save it for after you've been out hiking and the kids are a bit more ready to sit in the car. We also use car time to have our kids work on their Junior Ranger books. Find a way to make it enjoyable for your kids, and we know you will appreciate the scenery.

Second, have we mentioned the Gifford House pies? Along with those, if you're in the park during fruit-bearing season, head over to the Fruita Campground area and let your kids pick fruit. All of our kids, ages two to teen, got in on the apple-picking action. You can pick in designated orchards for free. It's a memory our kids have to this day.

Finally, if you've never had a chance to see rock art, as in pictographs and petroglyphs, this is the place to do it. Actually, even if you have, they never get old. (Get it? They're already old, but we never tire of seeing them!) Capitol Reef has a great area for viewing multiple examples of Fremont Culture petroglyphs up close and in a location everyone can access. Find the hike description in the Capitol Reef chapter to see how your whole family can experience the wonder of an ancient petroglyph.

Bryce Canyon National Park

Bryce is known for two things: hoodoos and dark night skies. Plan to take advantage of both while visiting this beautiful and unique area. You can take in the hoodoos best by hiking down among them. Our hiking trip descriptions will help you plan a way to do this that will work for your family. If you're non-hikers, this park has excellent viewing opportunities from the road. If you take the scenic drive from the entrance at the north to Rainbow Point in the south, stopping along the way, you will have many chances to see beautiful parts of the hoodoo canyons.

When planning a visit to Bryce, you will want to make special plans around events based on the night sky, if possible. The clear air, combined with some amazing telescopes, allows you to view galaxies beyond our own, new stars being birthed inside nursery nebulae, globular clusters like strings of diamonds, shock waves from exploding stars, and more. Because of this,

Thor's Hammer is one of the many hoodoos on the Navajo Loop Trail.

Bryce Canyon has a specialized ranger force found nowhere else: The Dark Rangers! These rangers are experts in all things celestial. They lead night hikes, give ranger talks focused on the skies, and even let you use their telescopes to view the heavens at night. The Dark Rangers will guide you and your kids in using the telescopes and finding events and objects to view in the night skies. The viewing is best when the skies are darkest, which is when the moon is smallest. If you visit when the moon is full, you will have a harder time seeing celestial events, but you might opt instead for a full-moon hike guided by a ranger. If all of that seems too much for your family, just taking time to gaze at the skies from your campsite will allow you to see more stars than you've probably seen in your life. This is, after all, one of the darkest places on earth! Check the astronomy programs schedule on the park website and make sure to plan time to experience the darkest night skies you quite possibly will ever see.

The other main attraction at Bryce is the hoodoos, natural rock formations sometimes called spires, towers, or pinnacles. They are formed by the freeze-thaw cycle of water, which breaks off large chunks of rock. Although hoodoos are found in smaller formations elsewhere, nowhere are the numbers and colors as spectacular as they are at Bryce. Bryce has some excellent options for hiking above and also down among the hoodoos; it even has a special program called "I Hiked the Hoodoos!" Check at the visitor center before heading out into the park for specific details, but it basically consists of hiking a certain number of miles and taking photos or rubbings (using a pencil and paper to rub over a metal emblem) at various locations. When you return with your evidence of having hiked the hoodoos, they will present you with a very nice metal pin. This incentive spurred our boys on when their energy was waning. In the Bryce Canyon Hiking Trips section, we share some of our best suggestions for how to get up close and personal with hoodoos and how to best enjoy them with your kids.

One other thing to keep in mind as you plan a trip to Bryce: the high elevation will make your stay substantially colder than a visit to another desert park. On a recent trip we went from hot and sweaty in Zion to very cold and shivering in Bryce. If you're planning on camping in Bryce, make sure you're prepared with warm sleeping bags and appropriate clothing. If you'll be going out at night for stargazing or a moonlight hike, you will want to really bundle up. You'll be surprised by how cold it can get once the sun goes down. Remember that kids' bodies are significantly smaller than adults' and they get colder much more easily. A cold kid is a fussy, whining kid. Keep those kids warm!

Finally, if you're on an extended national park trip in southwestern Utah and need showers and laundry, Bryce is the easiest place to do it. You will want to plan your trip so that you're at Bryce toward the middle of it and can take advantage of these facilities. Don't forget to bring quarters! We found the showers to be very generous with the amount of hot water a quarter buys, but the laundry dryers were a bit more expensive. It sure feels great after a few nights or a week of camping to have a hot shower and get into some clean clothes. Remember to leave a bit of time in your schedule to use these amenities!

Zion National Park

In order to fully understand the magnitude and scale of Zion Canyon, it's essential to experience two aspects of the park: the Virgin River and a hike to a higher vantage point. You will find various options for each of these in the Zion Hiking Trips section. The Virgin River is the beautiful and clear river that carved out this majestic canyon. As you walk along its banks, it can be hard to imagine that this sweet and calm stream is, at times, a rock-carving raging torrent. Throughout your travels in the park, you will learn how this river has shaped more than just rock. It has been instrumental in supporting both the human and animal life that have called this canyon home. While you're down along the river, you may have a hard time fully understanding the scale of the walls surrounding you. Once you begin to hike up and out of the canyon, you quickly gain an appreciation for the magnitude of Zion Canyon. Although many of the hikes up the sides of the canyon are considered strenuous, we think there are possibilities for your family. While planning your trip, make time for hikes along the river and up the sides of the canyon.

RAFTING IN SOUTHERN UTAH

If you have the time, you should consider taking advantage of the unique rafting experiences available in this part of the West. The Green River flows north to south out of Wyoming, and the mighty Colorado flows east to west out of its namesake state, joining together at the southern edge of Canyonlands National Park. See Resources for contact details.

Colorado River: Fisher Towers Section (starting near Moab)
An extremely popular and accessible rafting experience near Moab is what's called "the daily" on the Colorado River up State Highway 128. Almost all the local rafting companies offer half- or full-day guided trips in a variety of crafts.

Colorado River: Cataract Canyon (starting near Moab)
Before its confluence with the Green, the Colorado River has carved out Cataract Canyon, which offers 46 miles of world-class whitewater. The most intense section is 14 miles long and offers rapids that can range up to Class V, depending on river flows, meaning that this is not a river suitable for younger kids. Its remote and challenging nature requires expert-level abilities and equipment, as well as permits from

the National Park Service. However, numerous guide services offer trips ranging from two to six days long, depending on the needs of your group. If you search Cataract Canyon rafting trips online, you will be on your way to planning a memorable adventure.

Colorado River: Westwater Canyon (starting near Moab)
This section of the Colorado is shorter than the Cataract section and offers day trips for families with children ten and older. Like the Cataract Canyon, it's not recommended for younger children due to the challenging rapids.

Green River: Desolation and Gray Canyons (near the town of Green River)
This section of the Green River takes you through the isolated and historic Tavaputs Plateau. Once you enter this canyon, you're committed for the next 85 miles of river, and the trip will take four to six days. This river is suited to younger children, because its rapids land in the Class II–III range, but its scenery is definitely first class! It features beautiful red-rock canyon walls, Native American ruins, excellent hiking options, and amazing rock-art sites. Since most of the water is calm, it's often publicized as Utah's most popular family river vacation.

Rafting on the Green River (ROAM Family Travel/Tina Davis photo)

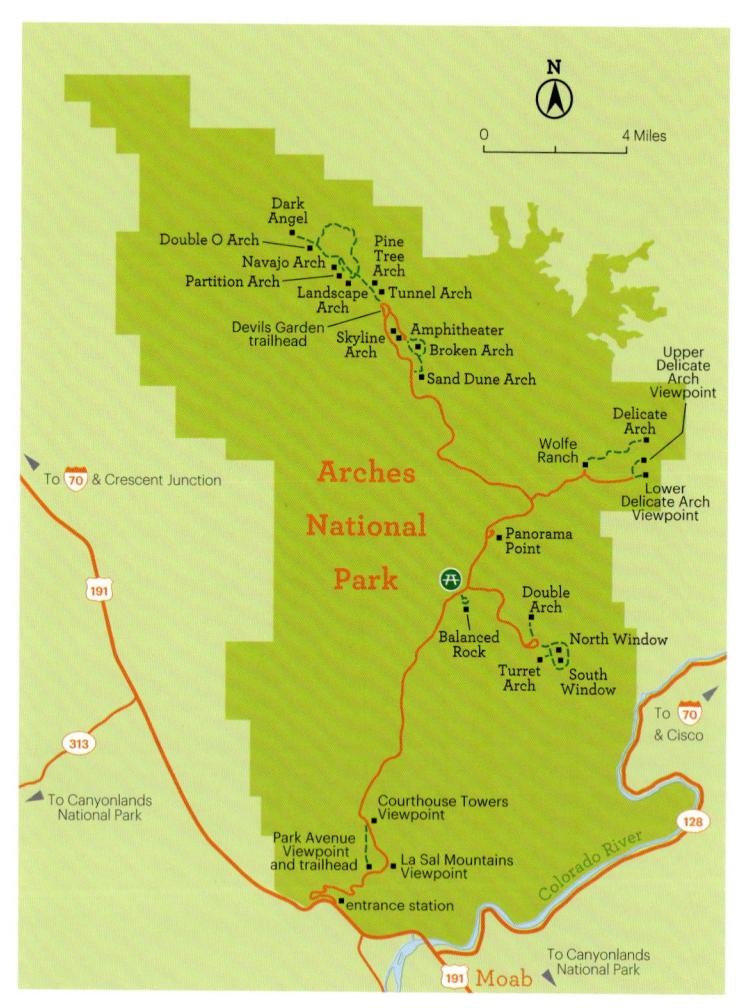

If you would like more detail, online versions of the map, which allow the user to zoom in and out, are available on the National Parks website for Arches.

ARCHES NATIONAL PARK

Abby explored Arches National Park as a child, and just one short trip there left a lasting impression. She remembers delicate soaring rock arch formations reaching across the sky above her, impossibly balanced sculptures that no man had made, and the otherness of the desert ecosystem heretofore unknown to her. She always longed to return. This longing, stretching over decades, is what inspired our family to visit this jewel of a national park in the fall of 2014. As we contemplated the best way to impress upon our children the importance of their personal heritage in the National Park System, we could think of no better place than Arches.

Why Arches? Think like a child for a moment. Children are captivated by mystery, enchantment, imagination. Why do you think Disney is so successful with our kids? They capture these qualities in their parks and movies, aimed at kids! Although we have been to most of the national parks west of the Mississippi, few compare to the mystery, enchantment, and imagination-boosting formations in Arches. Those formations were indelibly impressed upon Abby's young-girl mind, compelling her to find a way to take our children there decades later. And do you know what? She found herself experiencing the same sense of wonder as a grown adult that she had found as a child. Maybe we all are seeking some mystery and enchantment to kick-start our imaginations!

Arches National Park has more than two thousand arches in addition to soaring pinnacles, sandstone fins, and giant balanced rocks. Once you drive the long climb onto the park's upper plateau, you find that many of these exist along very accessible and mostly level trails, making this a great park for kids and older people. The proximity to the town of Moab also makes logistics a bit easier. Camping stores and excursion companies help ease the strain that camping can sometimes have on a family.

Now for a little bit of arch education! In order for an opening to be classified as an arch, it must be at least three feet wide. If you happen to discover a new arch, you get to name it. That little tidbit can keep your kids happily exploring for hours! New arches are constantly forming from fins of sandstone, and each year arches are deteriorating, moving toward eventual collapse. Abby clearly remembers seeing Wall Arch when she went to Arches as a young person, but when she returned with the kids decades later, it was gone. This dramatically reinforced the need to get our kids into the parks as soon as possible. We told them there were things they would see that their children never would.

When you first arrive at Arches, you will find the visitor center at the base of towering rock walls, and you will see the road into the park snaking back and forth up the face of these cliffs. Before you climb this road, you won't see any indication of the fantastic arches that await you. It's a good idea to make a brief stop at the visitor center before you set out to explore. However, we do not recommend you begin your park stay with a thorough tour of the visitor center. Your children will find the exhibits and park movie much more interesting after they have seen the arches for themselves. As adults we like to do a lot of research first, but kids want to discover things for themselves. After they have seen the arches, they find it much more meaningful to read the exhibits, and they love to see the arches they explored in the video. So we recommend a quick initial stop that allows you to pick up maps and the park newspaper (these are separate publications; at some parks they give you both up front and at others you need to request each one). The park newspaper gives you details about ranger programs, weather, road closures, and some hiking trails. You should also get the materials for the Junior Ranger program and an Explorer Pack if you choose to (more details on these are in tip number four in 5 Tips for

Landscape Arch has the widest span of any in the Arches National Park.

Making the Most of Your Utah Vacation, in the introduction to this book).

The visitor center at Arches has a unique feature our kids particularly liked. The back wall is made up of floor-to-ceiling windows that allow you to view the sandstone cliff you drive to the top of when you enter the park. Big binoculars are mounted to stands, and plaques describe various features of the rock wall. Our kids enjoyed looking through the binoculars and spent quite a while playing "I Spy" with each other. The interpretive displays are very well done and interesting, but we recommend you leave exploring these until the end of your stay.

A note about the layout of the park's trails: you will see on a map or in the descriptions below that many arches lie along a trail to another arch. It can be very tempting to think "Well, we've come this far along the trail; we should keep going and see the arches that are farther out." Although in some ways this is the most efficient way to plan your hikes, keep in mind that it can get you to a point where you're far from the end of your hike, but your kids don't feel they can go on. In the hiking

Greeting card shot, anyone?

section below, we give you some of our thoughts on when to give in and when to push on. Remember, efficiency isn't always the best goal!

Most of the famous rock formations are easily accessible via level, hard-packed trails that meander through sagebrush and large fins of sandstone. A few trails are a bit more challenging, due either to the distance or some required rock scrambling. Please keep in mind that you will be in a desert environment, so be sure to check out our 5 Tips for Making the Most out of Your Utah Vacation in the introduction.

GETTING TO ARCHES

Arches National Park is only 5 miles from Moab, Utah, but Moab isn't serviced by major air, train, or bus lines. You will need a car to move through the park, so if you will be flying in, plan on renting a car at the airport.

By car

From the north (starting from either east or west), you will be coming in on I-70, a major interstate. Turn south on US Highway 191 and drive 18 miles to the entrance of the park. Moab is just 5 miles farther.

If arriving from the south (e.g. the Grand Canyon or Monticello, Utah), find US 191 and follow it north through Moab and on to the entrance of the park.

By air

Arches is 110 miles southwest of Grand Junction, Colorado; 360 miles southwest of Denver, Colorado; and 236 miles south of Salt Lake City, Utah.

Whatever mode you choose to travel, we hope your time is spent mostly *outside* your vehicle!

ARCHES HIKING TRIPS

One of the best ways to help your kids enjoy their time in the park is by getting out on the trail. While hiking, your children will find a variety of ways to interact with nature and form a connection that will last for a lifetime. The following hiking trips offer your family some great choices for getting out of the car and into a personal experience with the world around them. Use the hiking descriptions to fill in your itinerary.

Sand Dune Arch

A short hike to a secluded feature with a lot of places for kids to scramble up and over rock formations. It's also a welcome

Baby gets out of the backpack to enjoy some playtime in the sand.

relief from the hot sun, because this narrow canyon stays shady and cool!

Distance: 0.3 mile roundtrip
Time: 15–20 minutes
Starting point: Sand Dune Arch parking area, in the northern part of the park

---

This short and easy hike is one of our favorites! You begin on a wide, hard-packed trail. Very soon you will see a sign directing you to leave the main trail and follow another path a short distance to the arch. The trail approaches a crevice between two rock fins, about 15 feet wide, and then heads inside. It begins to feel like you're in a stone room! There's another, smaller fin running through the crevice, and our kids had fun climbing up it and walking along the top. This is such a short hike that you really can afford to just let your kids explore.

When they've exhausted that fun, continue down the crevice until you have to bend right. The arch is tucked away in a little box canyon straight ahead of you. Although you must stay off the arch itself, there are many other fun rocks to climb around on and excellent sand to play in.

This is a great hike to do in the afternoon on a hot day, as it stays quite cool down in the "canyon" by the arch. Bring a snack and some sand toys and your children can spend a very pleasant afternoon here. If you're visiting Arches in a cooler time of year, you will want to bring at least sweatshirts to cover up with. If a small breeze starts up while you're there, it can get quite chilly!

Note that you can either do this hike by itself and be finished or head back to the main trail and continue on to Broken Arch and Tapestry Arch. See the map and hike details below for more information. Continuing on makes this hike longer than you may expect. Make sure you leave enough time so you won't be caught out in the desert as the sun is going down! If you want to extend your hike just a little bit, you can head out toward Broken

Arch and then return the way you came instead of following the lollipop loop around to Tapestry Arch.

Broken Arch–Tapestry Arch Loop Trail

A moderate trail that involves some routefinding on the return and includes interesting rock formations to navigate. If this sounds daunting, simply visit Broken Arch, then return the way you came.

Distance: 1.3 miles roundtrip from Sand Dune Arch trailhead or 2 miles if you hike the entire loop
Time: 30–60 minutes
Starting point: Sand Dune Arch parking area or Devils Garden Campground

---

Although you can start this trail in two different locations, we recommend that you leave from the Sand Dune Arch trailhead and parking area. The trail is much more clear and easy to find from this direction. If you choose to go in this direction, you will start out on a wide and hard-packed trail. Soon you leave that (just after the Sand Dune Arch turnoff) and meander across a delightful meadow of bunch grass. If the wind is blowing just a little you may find yourself feeling as though you're walking on water as the grasses sway back and forth. We saw jackrabbits and plenty of lizards on this stretch of the trail.

After you cross the meadow, you will have to do a bit of trail finding as you bend right and follow the rocks and a dry creek you find there. Follow these around and look for rock cairns marking the way. We weren't always sure we were on the trail, but once we got to the arch, we realized how hard it would be to get truly lost at this point. You see the arch ahead of you and then head down through a dry wash and up to the arch on the other side. From the inside of the arch, beautiful views reach far across the desert to the mountains beyond.

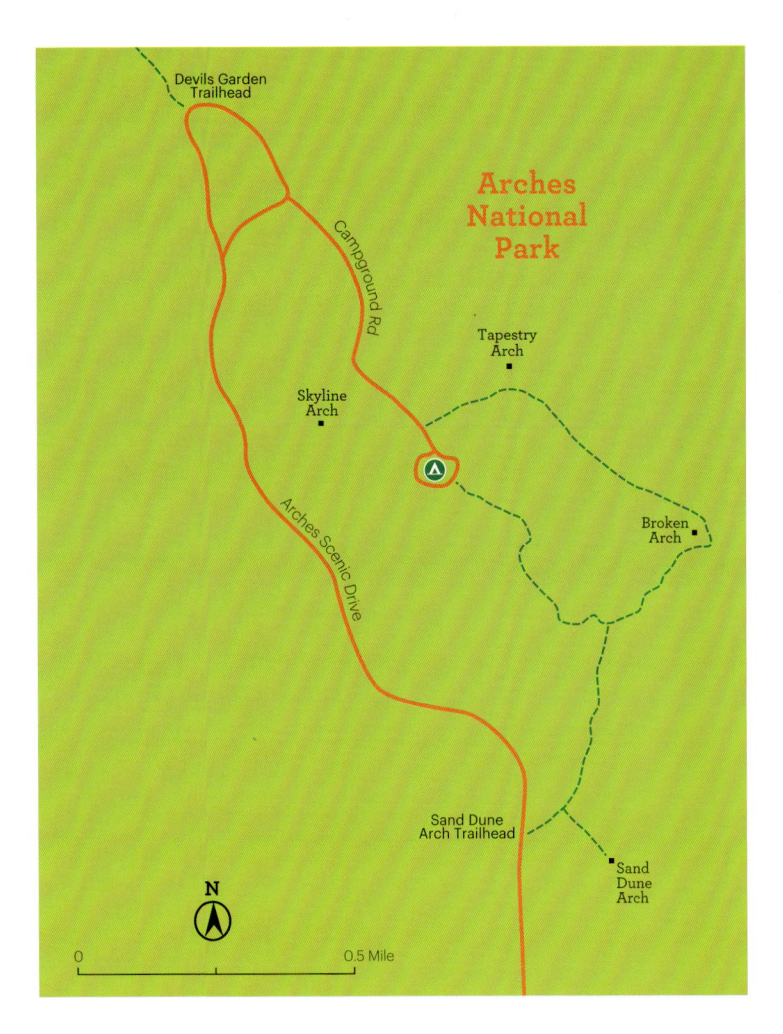

After spending some time at the arch, you can either proceed on to Tapestry Arch or head back the way you came. Unless you have older (teen) or really fit kids and plenty of time, or are staying in the campground, we suggest you head back. The trail

ARCHES NATIONAL PARK 53

How often do you get to cross a meadow with a view like this?

from here becomes very easy to lose and although it takes you to the campground, if your car isn't there, you will still have to complete the remaining two-thirds of the loop in order to get back to where you parked. Our kids found it tedious to have seen the main attractions (the arches) but still have so much farther to walk.

Pine Tree and Tunnel Arches

Short side spurs on the trail to Landscape Arch reveal two interesting arches and maybe a little bit more.

Distance: 1.5 miles roundtrip along the main trail with two 0.25-mile spurs to see the arches
Time: 20 minutes
Starting point: Devils Garden trailhead

Just a short jaunt down the trail toward Landscape Arch lies a side trail with a T-intersection at the end. To the right is Tunnel Arch and to the left is Pine Tree Arch. The main trail is hard-packed dirt and quite easy walking. You will have to descend a bit of a hill to reach the two arches, but the trail is firm and well maintained and shouldn't cause problems for most people.

Pine Tree Arch is a sweet arch with some nice shade at midday. We found boulders to rest on and spent a few quiet moments in contemplation here. Little kids will find good entertainment in the sandy bottom.

Tunnel Arch is much less approachable. Located high in a sandstone wall, it must be viewed from below. Kids find this much less interesting, but you may still want to check it out because this is where we found a great little seep full of fabulous animal tracks. A seep is a natural wet area where water wells up. Animals in the desert rely on these seeps. Your kids

Even if you don't see the animals themselves, their tracks are pretty exciting.

ARCHES NATIONAL PARK   55

have a good chance of seeing some great animal prints here, and if you're out around dawn or dusk and have the patience to sit still and watch, you may be rewarded with seeing the actual animals themselves!

Landscape Arch (on the Devils Garden Trail)

A classic of the park and possibly the widest arch you will ever see! The hike to Landscape Arch is easy, with a good trail that anyone can navigate. For the adventurous, continue on to Double O Arch (details below).

Distance: 1.6 miles roundtrip
Time: 30–60 minutes
Starting point: Devils Garden trailhead in the north of the park

Landscape Arch is an iconic ribbon of rock, impossibly spanning a distance more than a football field in width. It lies along a relatively flat stretch of gravel-surfaced trail that almost anyone can easily negotiate. It also offers short side trips to Pine Tree and Tunnel arches (see above). This trail is very popular, and even in the off-season you can expect to find it busy. This should not deter you, however, as the arch is spectacular. You won't be able to get as close to it as you can with many other arches, but that hardly matters; its sheer size would make it hard to take in if you were up too close.

After viewing Landscape Arch, you can either turn back the way you came or continue on toward Double O Arch (see below) and Dark Angel. Keep in mind that the terrain gets much more difficult to maneuver once you pass Landscape Arch and begin the primitive trail. You may well have another hour or more of hiking to get out to Double O Arch, and then you have to return all the way back. It may not be wise to continue unless you've already planned for it, you have enough water, and everyone is feeling really good.

Double O Arch (Devils Garden Trail with side hikes to Partition and Navajo Arches)

Our favorite hike in the park! Scrambling up steep stone inclines, walking along narrow fins of rock, side hikes to arches with stunning views, and plenty for both kids and adults to enjoy.

Distance: 4.2 miles roundtrip
Time: 2–3 hours
Starting point: Devils Garden trailhead at the north end of the park

The park service classifies this as a strenuous trail, but we found that the rewards more than offset the effort required. It requires scrambling over boulders, traversing sandstone faces, and being able to ignore minor heights, but it's also moderate in terms of overall elevation gain and comes with views that inspire. We went with a baby in a backpack, a nine-year-old, an eleven-year-old, and a thirteen-year-old. Admittedly, our boys are great at rock scrambling, so be sure to make an honest assessment of

Navajo Arch is a great spot for a cool rest on a hot day.

Desert solitude

your family members' individual abilities. If you're all ready for this hike, you will have an amazing time.

You begin at the same trailhead as you would for Landscape Arch; in fact, you hike to Landscape Arch and then continue on. The trail to Landscape Arch is well used and hard packed, but it becomes much more primitive once you pass the arch. The trail first becomes sandy, making for tiring walking, and then rocky and boulder strewn. This is where it started to get fun for our kids (and for us too!). The trail heads out over huge fins of sandstone that you must traverse, ascend, or travel around. The trail is easy to follow, and you will likely find people all along the way at any time of year. At the tops of a few of the fins, you will find breathtaking scenery with views reaching to the faraway mountains. Make sure to allow time to take it all in.

Along the way you will see signs for short hikes to two side arches, Partition and Navajo. These are worth a diversion, so hang a left and check them out. Navajo Arch lies in a secluded alcove in a fin of sandstone. It's cool in there and a great place for a rest. Our boys were tempted by a good-sized pool of water in the sand underneath the arch, but it's really best not to disturb these potholes (the technical name for them). These pools provide water for a variety of desert critters who don't appreciate the oils that sunscreen contain—and even plain human sweat can be bad for the tiny creatures who call these potholes home.

Partition Arch will give you expansive views through both a large arch and a smaller opening to its right.

After checking out all those arches, proceed to Double O Arch farther on. As you near the end you may be wondering where the arch is hiding, but the final approach takes you along a fin rising far above the floor below. There is evidence of many dropped items in the cracks below, so hold on to your stuff and your kids! As you cross this large fin, look left to catch a glimpse of Double O Arch and then make your way down to a sandy area with scattered juniper bushes and find a spot to rest and snack. We did a few of our Family Explorer pack activities, and our kids had fun running around the back sides of the arches and scaling the rock to either side. Remember: you're not permitted to walk out on the actual arches.

From here it's another half mile out to Dark Angel. Having visited it before, and after all the fun we'd already had, we decided not to add the extra mile to our kids' feet on our most recent trip. For those with the stamina, Dark Angel is a well-recognized standing monolith made famous by rock climbers. Once you've had your fill, turn around and head back the way you came.

Delicate Arch

The first part of the hike is hot and boring, but the payoff at the end is a sublime view of perhaps the region's most iconic sight. This hike is strenuous, best for fit older kids and adults.

Distance: 3 miles roundtrip
Time: 2–3 hours plus time for pictures at the destination
Starting point: Wolfe Ranch parking area

An old homesteader's cabin

Delicate Arch: you've seen it on brochures, screen savers, license plates, and postcards, and now you can see it in person. You actually have two options to view it, the first being a viewing platform you can drive to. This vantage point is about a thousand yards, or two-thirds of a mile, from the arch, with a modest backdrop. If you're willing to burn a little boot leather, you can hike to the view that made it famous and actually stand underneath the arch while the formation frames a gorgeous view of the distant snow-clad La Sal Mountains.

We'll be honest and tell you up front that this isn't our favorite hike in Arches (especially the beginning two-thirds), but the payoff is worth it. In addition, at the very beginning of the trail are an old homestead cabin and some Native American petroglyphs that always spark a child's imagination. So if you can afford the time and effort, we're pretty sure you won't be disappointed.

After the hike leaves the parking area, you immediately come to an old homestead cabin made of logs. Go ahead and ask

Watch your step!

your kids where the Wi-Fi router and TV went in this old house. Then continue a little farther and take a short side trail to view ancient Native American petroglyphs.

The hike meanders through a fairly barren desert wash for quite a bit before beginning to climb up a massive slab of rock. The rock is huge and has a flat surface the equivalent of several football fields that climbs gradually but continually upward for a surprising distance. You will be fully exposed to the sun the entire time and likely huffing a bit from the climb, but even in this uncomfortable situation, it's hard not to be amazed at the sheer immensity of the rock you're standing on.

As you reach the top, the trail wanders through narrow, shallow canyons and gets more interesting as you go. There are shallow ephemeral potholes in them after a recent rain, and the trail is sand and dirt as opposed to stone, at least for a time. Eventually you find yourself strolling along a veritable sidewalk of stone hewn out of the massive rock formation that leads to Delicate Arch, and you have impressive views of the surrounding terrain to the left side—at least if you're able to look past the steep drop-off at the trail's edge. Before long you come to a saddle in the rock formation and, looking to your right and across an open bowl, you see the view that has inspired so many photographers.

You will likely see a number of aspiring photographers all over the area and may find it difficult to get a picture of the formation on its own. But it's so large, the presence of a few tourists doesn't seem to detract from images much as long as you're prepared for the inevitable crowds. Once you're past the last portion of the hike, with its steep drop-off, you will likely feel relatively safe at the final destination. But the bowl immediately in front of the arch is surprisingly steep, so keep an eye on your kids and be clear about where they can and cannot go. We've seen dropped water bottles go flying down this hill to land in the sandy bottom, something we'd never wish to see happen to an adult, let alone a child. So be a little vigilant around Delicate Arch.

Park Avenue

Best if you have someone to pick you up at the other end, this is an easy hike through a dry wash that takes you through the heart of an inspiring canyon. Go early or late in the day to get some shade.

Distance: 1 mile one way (recommended)
Time: 30–60 minutes
Starting point: Either the Park Avenue Viewpoint (recommended) or the Courthouse Towers Viewpoint

---

This was one of the last things we did in Arches because we were having trouble deciding if it would be worth it. After all, we came to see arches, and the Park Avenue Trail doesn't have any. We had a bit of extra time on our last day, so we decided to check it out. The verdict? It's worthwhile if you can make the time.

Great options for boulder-hopping along Park Avenue

If you decide to hike it, we highly recommend doing it in one direction, from the Park Avenue Viewpoint in the southernmost part of the park toward the Courthouse Towers Viewpoint farther to the north. A long stone staircase at the trailhead descends to the valley below. You will be happy you chose to go down and not up it! There is no park shuttle, so hiking this in one direction only meant Abby dropped everyone off and drove around to meet them at the other end. If your driver wants a little bit of the Park Avenue experience, we recommend taking a few moments at the trailhead to walk out on the stone viewing area and look down through the valley. Then, when you reach the pick-up area, park and walk over and into the "avenue" until you meet up with your family. Then you can all hike out together.

The trail itself is aptly named. After descending the staircase, you find yourself on a solid rock riverbed that is wide and flat, resembling in many ways an actual avenue. Walk down this stone avenue between opposing towering rock fins for the majority of the trail. From your vantage point on the valley floor, you see interesting patterns in the rock layers, fascinating shapes on the tops of the fins, and rocks perfectly sized to climb on and jump off. Kids will love the feeling of this hike. The towering fins give you some shade early and late in the day, so plan accordingly.

North and South Windows and Turret Arch

A short and easy loop to some of the park's most accessible and impressive arches.

Distance: 1 mile roundtrip (all on gravel trail)
Time: 30–60 minutes
Starting point: Windows parking area adjacent to Double Arch parking in the middle of the park

---

This group of three arches is an easy way to get a feel for what this park represents in a short amount of time. After parking in

Turret Arch beckons from the Windows.

the large lot, head out on the slightly rising gravel trail toward the arches. You come to a split in the trail, and at this point it becomes a loop. Travel in either direction around the loop to see the massive arches. The two window arches are interesting, but we had much more fun at Turret Arch. You can get right up inside the arch and climb around to the back side easily. There were plenty of rock-scrambling opportunities here, and we all enjoyed our stop.

Double Arch

Leaving from the other side of the parking lot above, this is another short and easy hike to an accessible and impressive arch.

Distance: 0.5 mile roundtrip (all on gravel trail)
Time: 30 minutes
Starting point: Double Arch parking area adjacent to Windows parking in the middle of the park

---

This delightful hike leads to a grand but approachable arch. You walk along a hard-packed, sandy trail with a crowd of other visitors for a short distance to a big, round archway. At the foot of the arch you find its sandstone base rising up off the valley floor. You can scale this fairly easily if you want to get right up in the arch or look out through it. Just remember that it's always easier to go up than to come back down and that sandstone can be very slick when wet.

This short hike is easily combined with the Windows arches and Turret Arch. Simply cross the parking lot into the upper lot and locate the trailhead. Neither hike is long or strenuous, so this is a good chance to "bag" a bunch of arches in a short time. All of these hikes are very exposed, so plan to hike during the cooler part of the day and take the usual precautions for hiking in the sun.

OTHER ACTIVITIES IN ARCHES

The main attractions at Arches National Park are, well, the arches. This park is fascinating in its unusual geology but pretty undeveloped as parks go. There is only one campground, and there are no facilities for horseback riding. The lack of rivers in the park makes boating activities nonexistent within its boundaries. However, there are rafting options nearby, so if you want to make a whitewater raft trip part of your journey, see Rafting in Southern Utah in the Best Bets chapter.

Wildlife viewing

Although the desert may at times appear barren, that is simply not true at all. The reason people often don't see wildlife in Arches is that animals living in desert ecosystems such as this have to live a little differently than animals in a more temperate ecosystem. The heat and aridity of Arches mean you're most likely to see wildlife at dawn or dusk. One way to boost your chances: if you find a small pothole or area of wet sand during the day, come back to that area in the evening or early the next

A collared lizard (NPS/Neal Herbert photo)

morning. Sit a respectable distance away and wait quietly; you may be rewarded with a sighting. We found one such wet area at the base of a tree growing at the foot of a tall sandstone wall, just to the left before the entrance to Sand Dune Arch. We clearly saw many animal tracks in the mud. Many small children find it hard to sit still waiting for wildlife, and many teenagers find it boring, so often our kids just enjoy looking for signs of animals instead. Animals you may see—or at least see the tracks of—include rodents like chipmunks, pack rats, and kangaroo rats; birds such as hawks, eagles, and songbirds; and other animals including lizards, coyotes, jackrabbits, and deer.

Rock climbing

There is some excellent rock climbing in Arches, but much of it is advanced. Unless you're a proficient climber, we don't recommend taking kids climbing on your own. Also, if you're planning to climb, keep in mind that the park requires you to get a free permit ahead of time and that certain climbing areas may be closed to protect nesting birds. Make sure to check in with a park ranger before doing any climbing, and be aware of all the best practices and regulations specific to this park. See the park's website for more infomation.

Bicycling

Bicycling is not allowed on trails or in undeveloped areas of Arches. You may ride bikes on the roads, but they are quite narrow, often with no shoulder, and full of tourists busy looking at arches and not watching for kids on bikes! We don't recommend bike riding for kids in this park. However, Moab is a mecca for mountain biking, and you will see a lot of folks with fat-tire bicycles heading out of town. So while this attraction is not really about the park and therefore outside the scope of this book, you can find a lot of information with a quick internet search if you're interested in going on a mountain bike excursion in this famous locale.

Backpacking

Due to the park's limited size, it has relatively few backcountry areas. As of 2017, the National Park Service has new backcountry camping guidelines for Arches, so check the park website for updates on getting permits. Rangers can also fill you in about stipulations on where you can camp. We only recommend desert backpacking with kids to very fit parents, as the lack of water means you will be carrying a lot of extra weight. If you choose to go, however, you will be rewarded with expansive, starry, and cool desert nights.

ARCHES CAMPING AND LODGING

Due to its relatively small size, Arches has very few options for camping and lodging.

Lodges

There are no lodges in Arches National Park. If you wish to lay your head in a bed, you can find options in the nearby town of Moab. An internet search will give you many options.

Campgrounds

There is only one campground in Arches, Devils Garden Campground. It has fifty sites that are usually fully occupied from March through September; you will have to make reservations far ahead of time to score one. The campground has picnic tables, potable water, grills, and both pit and flush toilets. There are no Recreational Vehicle (RV) hook-ups or showers. As of publication time, sites are $20 per night.

The park's close proximity to a good-sized town, Moab, makes staying off-site a good option. We took this opportunity to find a place in town with laundry and showers. Since Bryce Canyon National Park is the only national park in Utah to have laundry and showers, getting clean can be difficult on an extended trip. If you choose to camp off-site, or are forced to due to lack of availability, this is the park to do it. Your trip into the park will only take ten to fifteen minutes, and you will enjoy those little extra comforts!

There are also some designated campsites along the Colorado River to the south of the park. These are first come, first served, but if you get there early on a weekday, you might have a chance at one of those.

CAMPSITES IN MOAB:

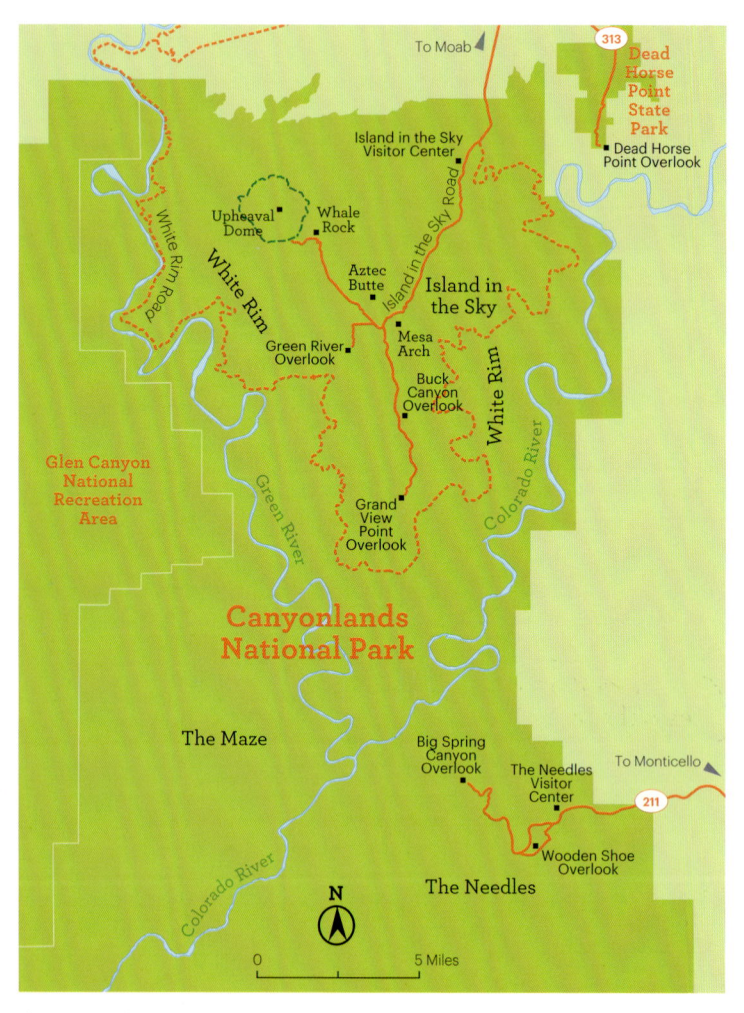

If you would like more detail, online versions of the map, which allow the user to zoom in and out, are available on the National Parks website for Canyonlands.

CANYONLANDS NATIONAL PARK

Canyonlands National Park is at the intersection of two iconic rivers of the west, the Green River and the Colorado River. As shifting tectonic plates lifted this plateau of land ever higher, the rivers in turn gashed this dry landscape ever deeper in twisting, tortured canyons of rock and soil to create the unique topography here today. How does a desert landscape produce such mighty rivers? The waters here originate hundreds of miles away in the mountainous regions of western Colorado and Wyoming and continue their journey for hundreds more through the Grand Canyon and beyond.

When we began planning our first trip to Canyonlands National Park, we had no idea that the park is divided into three distinct areas that are not easily accessible from one another. That's pretty important to know when you're deciding on activities and where to stay! As the Colorado River and the Green River make their ways across the park, they divide it into the three different units: Island in the Sky, The Needles, and The Maze; the rivers comprise a fourth park district. Each region has its own unique qualities, and it's important to understand them before you begin making detailed trip plans.

The Island in the Sky district is a mesa rising up between the two rivers. As you drive into this district from the north, you're given no clues as to how far the land falls away to meet the rivers down below. It isn't until you begin exploring this part of the park that you come to understand how it got its name. In this region you will find amazing vistas, a dramatic arch, starry nights, and more. This district is the easiest to explore if your time is limited or you're traveling with children, so it is the focus of our guide.

The Needles district is much more remote, with fewer services. Most of this region's stunning features are only accessible by desert backpacking or extreme four-wheel-drive roads. This area boasts a diverse landscape of desert arches and pinnacles, grassy meadows, and riverside habitat. Although it's a popular place to explore for people seeking solace and solitude, it's not ideal for trips with kids. If you choose to check out this region, please do so with much planning and preparation.

The final district is The Maze, and it's one of the nation's most remote areas! It's known for silence, isolation, and intense physical challenges. There are towers, buttes, mesas, and canyons to explore for the most self-reliant of outdoorspeople. One of the best-known hikes is through Horseshoe Canyon, where you find life-sized pictographs in a panel known as the Great Gallery. There is no water, and you will only find primitive campsites requiring a backcountry permit.

If you take our advice and limit your visit to the Island in the Sky district, you will still find many activities worth doing. Even with the limited hiking activities, there's plenty to enjoy!

A word of caution: the only water in the park is at the visitor center, quite a distance from most of the hiking attractions. It's near the entrance of the park, so you will want to fill up all water bottles there and maybe have some extra too. Note that the visitor center is not open in winter, so be sure to check the park website for current hours if you are planning a trip at that time of year. We hope you will make an effort to get your kids out of the car and into nature, and that goes a lot better if you bring plenty of water. Also, don't forget to bring along Junior Ranger booklets or Explorer Packs, which you can check out at the visitor center!

GETTING TO CANYONLANDS

Like Arches, Canyonlands is close to Moab, which is only 33 miles from the Island in the Sky Visitor Center. Unlike Arches, each of its districts is only accessible via a separate road. There are no bridges across the rivers, so you cannot access one district from another.

By car

From I-70, turn south on US Highway 191 toward Moab. To visit Island in the Sky, turn south on State Route 313 just north of Moab and drive about 20 miles to the park entrance.

For The Needles district, take US 191 south from Moab until you reach SR 211, which leads to The Needles.

If you're daring enough to plan an adventure in The Maze, you need to be prepared for rugged roads. The only roads that access this area are graded dirt or high-clearance, four-wheel-drive roads. They are impassable when wet, so check the weather before you go.

Big views await at Canyonlands National Park.

By air

Commercial airlines will deliver you to Grand Junction, Colorado, or Salt Lake City, Utah. These airports are at least two and four hours away from Island in the Sky, respectively. You may also be able to fly on a small commercial carrier from Denver or Salt Lake City to the Moab Airport (CNY).

ISLAND IN THE SKY HIKING TRIPS

This district of Canyonlands is characterized by a number of short but sweet hikes to amazing views. Below we provide more detail so that you can choose the ones that fit your family and timeline.

Mesa Arch

A short hike to an arch with a surprising vista.

Distance: 0.5 mile roundtrip
Time: 30 minutes, with added time to hang out and admire the view
Starting point: Mesa Arch trailhead near the Willow Flat Campground

---

This is a popular sunrise hike with stunning views of the La Sal Mountains. We highly recommend it for families of all ability levels. Even if you've just visited Arches National Park, don't be tempted to skip this arch. Although we love the arches in Arches, this rock span has something special to add: dramatic vistas!

The hike out to Mesa Arch is short and well worn. You will encounter loose soil and smaller rocks, but mostly you're hiking on large, flat stones that provide good footing. The trail is a short loop you can hike in either direction. Just follow the obvious path until you see the arch ahead of and slightly below you. As you approach, you begin to see the dramatic view through the arch as it perches on the cliff edge.

We allowed our kids to run ahead and scramble around on the trail but reined them in closer to the arch due to the huge

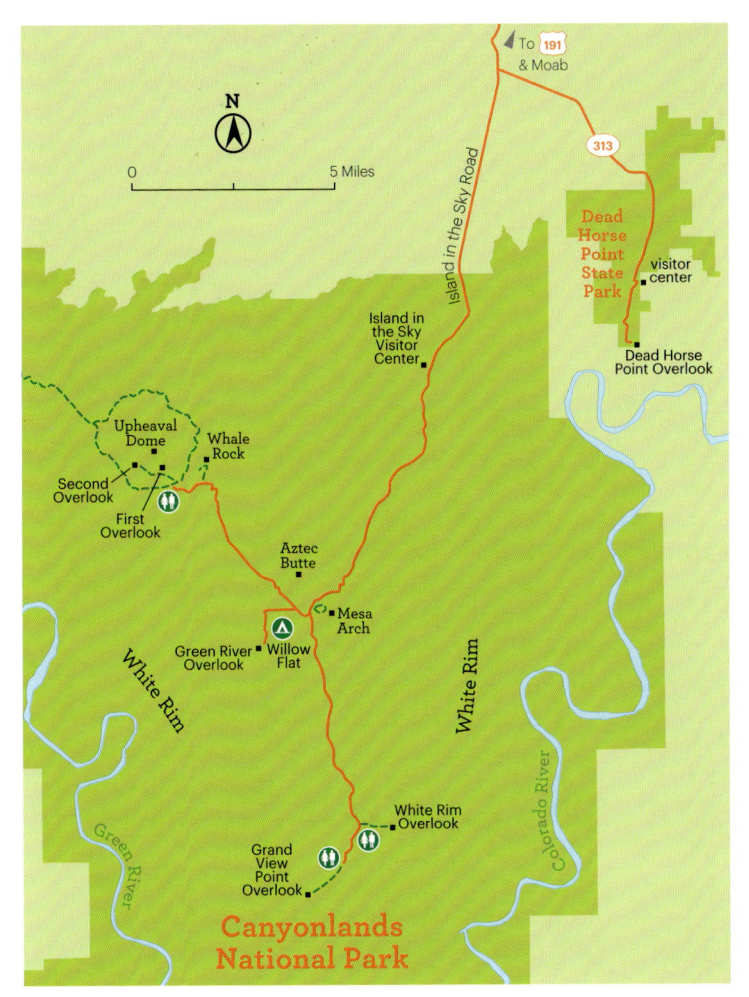

Island In The Sky

drop-off. After they enjoyed testing their bravery by climbing around near the arch and cliff edge, they joined a bunch of other kids playing in the large, flat area immediately before the arch.

CANYONLANDS NATIONAL PARK 75

The terrain falls away dramatically just beyond Mesa Arch.

Grand View Point

A well-traveled but worthwhile hike to some of the best views of the other regions of the park.

Distance: 2 miles roundtrip
Time: 1.5 hours
Starting point: Grand View Point Overlook trailhead at the southern end of Grand View Point Road

This is a spectacular hike that will really give you a feel for the scope of the park as a whole. It allows you to set off onto the mesa and follow the rim to its terminus point. It is mostly flat with good footing, and it's easy enough to stay back from the edge if you're worried about kids and sharp drop-offs. Also, if you or your kids get tired at any point, you can always just turn back.

As you leave the large and heavily used parking area (with its own views) and head out onto the mesa, you leave much of the crowd behind. The trail is mostly marked with rock cairns, but even where it isn't, it would be quite difficult to get lost. You're walking out onto a peninsula of stone that drops off on both sides, so it's impossible to wander too far from the trail, provided you don't jump off a cliff!

When you reach the narrowest part of this peninsula, you find yourself with views stretching out in all directions. From this point you can see the park's two other districts, The Maze and The Needles, although from this lofty vantage it's hard to really comprehend their scope. You are also able to see the confluence of the Green and Colorado rivers far below. Also observable at the point and along the way is the stunning geology shaped by the elements.

We took this as a ranger-led hike and highly recommend that. Our ranger was personable and knowledgeable and made the hike so much more than a path to an overlook. The group we went with was fairly large, but there's plenty of room to spread

You can't get the entire grand view in a single photo!

out around the ranger and hear what he or she has to share. We learned about geology, soil organisms, park history, and many other intriguing facts. I don't always feel ranger-led hikes are great for kids, but this one offers enough space and diversity of subject to keep them interested. Check in with the visitor center ahead of time and, if at all possible, schedule this hike with a ranger.

Upheaval Dome: First and Second Overlooks

A short hike to an impressive geologic anomaly.

Distance: 0.8 mile roundtrip for first overlook, 1.8 total roundtrip to both first and second
Time: 30 minutes roundtrip to the first overlook, 1 hour roundtrip to both the first and second
Starting point: Upheaval Dome trailhead and parking area, at the end of Upheaval Dome Road

---

This trail starts out with a bit of climbing, but it isn't long—less than ten minutes—before you reach the first overlook point. There, you are treated to sweeping views of a bizarre landscape that looks otherworldly, and in fact scientists still have not reached consensus on exactly what caused this unique geologic feature. Have your kids suggest ideas and let their imaginations run wild.

From this point it's an almost equal distance to the second overlook on an interesting trail, but the additional effort does not result in anything especially new. You get roughly the same view of the main Upheaval Dome feature as well as some views of the surrounding area to the west, but you already get plenty of this even from the road. If you have a little time and energy to tackle the second portion of the trail, by all means do it, but if you're pressed for time, the first overlook gives you the most bang for your buck.

You have to see Upheaval Dome's amazing colors and formations to believe them.

Whale Rock

A fun kids' hike where you get to scramble all over a massive stone. We did it at night to gaze at the stars and add to the adventure!

Distance: 1 mile roundtrip
Time: 1 hour
Starting point: Whale Rock pullout just before Upheaval Dome parking area

---

This hike involves a willingness to wander a bit if you aren't sure where the trail went! It combines a bit of meandering and some rock scrambling, and it ends with a great vista—either of scenery or, our favorite, the starry night sky.

Whale Rock is an enormous sandstone dome rising out of the desert sands. You begin by wandering around smaller boulders and plants until you reach the bottom of Whale Rock itself.

Then it's a bit of a scramble along the sandstone toward the top. Once there, you are rewarded with expansive views of the Island in the Sky district.

Remember we mentioned that views are often not enough for kids? Well, here they also get some rock scrambling, which they love. But if you're even more adventurous, you can surprise your offspring with a nighttime jaunt to the top of the rock! Be prepared for your kids to be a little creeped out while you're wandering in the dark. It's natural to be a little unsure of yourself when your sense of sight is diminished and your other senses are heightened. But it's such a good experience to encounter the desert at night using those other senses. Just be sure to stay on the trail, even while wandering in the dark; the cryptobiotic soil is alive and shouldn't be crushed! Once you're on top of the rock, prepare to be amazed. There are only a few small surrounding towns and they are far away, so the night sky in the desert is like no other. You might want to study up on constellations that will be visible or use one of the many apps that allow you to identify them. Another game we like to play is to each find our own picture in the stars and make up a story to go with it.

If you plan to go out at night, you will need flashlights, warmer clothes, and sturdy shoes with good tread. On evenings around a full moon you might not need a flashlight, but it's always nice to have one just in case. Also, knowing they have one can help scared kids feel better. Remember that even in the desert it can be quite cool at night, so dress appropriately. We went out on a clear October night and felt it was quite warm but still wore sweatshirts and jeans. Finally, you may want to scout the hike out during the daytime, as it can be quite hard to locate at night. We didn't do that and never actually made it to Whale Rock. Instead, we landed on the top of another sandstone dome along the trail and enjoyed the sky just as much as if we had been on the actual Whale Rock. Keep in mind as you try to find your way in the dark that the kids would rather just lay out on any old rock and enjoy the night skies than wander for an extended period looking for the "right" rock!

Green River Overlook

This is the best place in the park to observe sunset. Bring your camera!

Distance: A short walk from the parking area
Time: A few minutes
Starting point: Green River Overlook parking area, just past the Willow Flat Campground

---

If you're looking for a fabulous spot to watch the sun set over the park, look no farther than the Green River Overlook. Drive to the parking area (or walk if you're camped at Willow Flat), and choose a spot to watch the light change over the river valley as the sun sets. There are various places to sit and stand; our kids chose to climb up on the big sandstone outcropping that dominates the cliff edge. Get comfortable and enjoy the show! This would also be a great place to come watch the stars later at night.

It's worth timing it so you can catch sunset on the rocks at Green River Overlook.

OTHER ACTIVITIES IN CANYONLANDS

Hiking is great, but you have a few other options for enjoying the park as well.

Wildlife viewing

The high-desert climate of Island in the Sky makes it difficult to do much wildlife spotting. There are deer and bighorn sheep in the park, along with mountain lions and bobcats. Most of the wildlife is around the river corridors, which lie far below the Island in the Sky plateau.

Rock climbing

There are a few sanctioned rock climbing areas in the park. Most of the established routes are in Island in the Sky, as the quality of the rocks in the other districts is not sufficient for climbing. Keep in mind that in many areas climbing is prohibited due to the protected status of ancient ruins or artifacts. Choose established routes only. If you think you want to do some climbing, consult a climbing guidebook to find the best current, safe, and accessible routes for kids.

Bicycling

Canyonlands is famous for some of its mountain bike terrain, specifically the White Rim Road in the Island in the Sky district. Cyclists must stay on designated trails and need a permit for the White Rim, even on just a day trip. To do an overnight bike trip, you will need to pursue a permit well in advance here—see Resources. You will also need a backcountry camping permit.

White Rim Road stretches for 100 miles on the bench below the Island in the Sky mesa. You can see the road from the Grand View Point Overlook. In good weather conditions the road is easy in a few places and very challenging in others (sections of the Shafer Trail, Lathrop Canyon Road, Murphy Hogback, Hardscrabble Hill, and the Mineral Bottom Road switchbacks).

Whoop it up if you tackle the White Rim Road. (NPS/Neal Herbert photo)

Also, there is no potable water along the trail, so bring at least one gallon per person per day.

Biking is permitted in the rest of Island in the Sky district. Bicyclists on paved roads must ride single file with the flow of traffic. There are no designated bike lanes, and road shoulders are often narrow, so think carefully before you decide to bike with kids here.

Four-wheel-drive trips

For the adventurous family that owns or is willing to rent high-clearance four-wheel-drive vehicles, there are some great trails to explore. Hundreds of miles of roads take you to various backcountry campsites, trailheads, and views. White Rim Road in Island in the Sky is classified as moderate. It is 100 miles long and takes you around a shelf below the mesa. A low-range four-wheel-drive vehicle is required. Also, if you plan to camp, you will need a backcountry permit. These are reserved in advance at the NPS website—see Resources.

River rafting

Canyonlands National Park is the only desert park in this area to have river rafting within its boundaries. However, if you're visiting Island in the Sky district, the rivers are far, far below you and quite inaccessible. Still, we find river rafting to be a unique and wonderful way to experience nature. If you're interested in rafting, see the Rafting in Southern Utah section, which will help you find a commercial outfitter and give you some questions to ask when choosing a guide.

You know you've chosen well when you get a perfect site for some hammock-style relaxation.

CANYONLANDS CAMPING AND LODGING

Being as remote as it is, Canyonlands National Park does not have lodge or cabin options, but it does offer limited camping.

Willow Flat Campground

There is only one small campground, Willow Flat Campground, in the Island in the Sky district. It is a beautiful desert campground that exudes silence, solitude, and reflection. All twelve sites are first come, first served and fill up by midmorning from March through June and again from September through mid-October. We camped the night before in Arches National Park, which is a short half-hour drive away. We got up pretty early, packed up camp, and headed over to Canyonlands. We arrived at 9:00 AM and found a site, but the sites were all full shortly after at 9:45 AM.

The campground is just over 7 miles from the entrance to the park. The sites are basic, with fire pits/grates, picnic tables with wood pergolas, and vault toilets but no water. Our beloved camping hammocks immediately went up between the pergola uprights and relaxation set it! The sites can accommodate RVs up to 28 feet long. When you're camped here, you're only a short walk from one of the park's best sunset points, Green River Overlook.

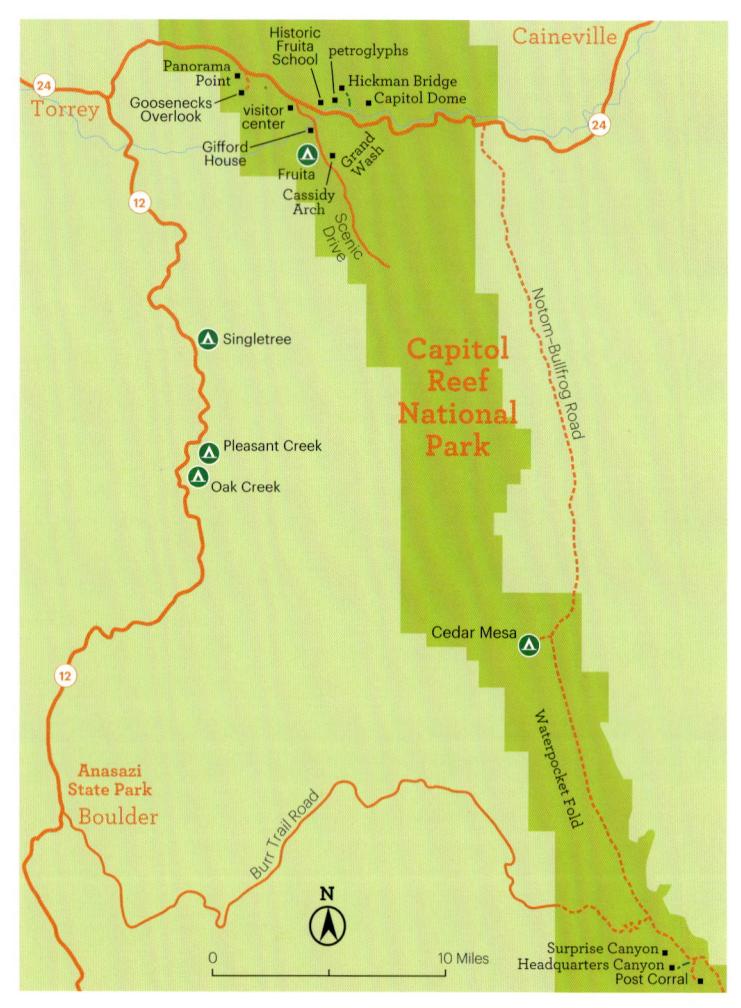

If you would like more detail, online versions of the map for Capitol Reef, which allow the user to zoom in and out, are available on the National Parks website.

CAPITOL REEF NATIONAL PARK

Throughout our time visiting national parks in Utah, we were constantly amazed that each park, no matter how close to another park, had its own distinct personality. Capitol Reef is no exception. Once again, as we entered and explored the park, we were fascinated by how different this park was from all the others. Capitol Reef is unique in its geology, its history, and the way it operates ... oh, and there's pie! More on that later.

The geologic feature that defines Capitol Reef and sets it apart from all the other national parks is called the Waterpocket Fold. The Waterpocket Fold is an enormous uprising of the earth's layers that runs from the top of the park to the bottom. A classic monocline, the fold has one extremely steep side caused by layers of earth on one tectonic plate pushing up over the top of another plate. The geology of this fold defines the park. It creates pockets that store rainwater, exposes layers of earth in a wide variety of colors, and produces a handful of arches. Only a few canyons cut all the way through its mass.

Although the geology is the most striking feature separating this park from the others, its historical sites quickly give you another reason to check it out. Because there are few passages through the Waterpocket Fold, the road that is now State Route 24 became a focus for settlers, Native peoples, cattle ranchers, and anyone else with reason to be traveling through. You see evidence of this activity in the many historical buildings in the Fruita Rural Historic District, near the visitor center, and the Fruita Campground. You will find old buildings, gardens, and orchards scattered throughout this area, as well as a good number of deer and wild turkeys.

All this and apples too! You can pick your own fruit at Fruita Campground.

The last major difference you may spot in Capitol Reef is the way it's run. First of all, you will not encounter a fee station as you drive in on SR 24. You're free to drive right on through if you choose. They ask that you stop in at the visitor center and pay a nominal fee of $10 per car if you plan to spend any time in the park. Did you get that? Only $10 per car—at least at the time of publication! It's not the normal park fee we're used to. You will find that other things are pretty laid back here too. The campgrounds are first come, first served, but because the Fruita Campground is so large and spacious, you don't feel as much pressure to get your site before they're all gone. Oh, and here's where the pie comes in. Fruita Campground is spread out under and between orchards bearing all kinds of fruit. Each year the fruit from those orchards is collected and turned into glorious pies sold at the historic Gifford House near the campground. This really was a highlight for our four boys. (Who are we kidding? We enjoyed it at least as much as they did!) The pies aren't cheap, but they're well worth the money. They have five or more flavors, and you can even buy ice cream to go along with them. We sat outside the Gifford House store in the sun, passing the pies and scooping up juicy, gooey bites of berry and apple sweetness. Many of the orchards are open to the public for free foraging in season. When we were there in the fall, our kids picked a huge bucketful of apples that we snacked on for days to come.

To fully enjoy your stay here, hike and explore its geology as you would in many other parks, but don't forget to make time for understanding its historic importance—and for eating pie!

GETTING TO CAPITOL REEF

Capitol Reef is unique among national parks in that a state highway goes right through the center of it. It's about midway between Bryce Canyon National Park and Moab (Canyonlands and Arches national parks), so there's no reason not to swing through Capitol Reef on your way from one side of the state to the other.

By car

Traveling westbound on I-70 from Canyonlands or Arches, take SR 24 west toward Hanksville (exit 149). Stay on SR 24 for 95 miles to reach the park visitor center.

If you are coming from the west, you are most likely heading from Zion or Bryce Canyon. In either case, get on SR 12 and follow that east through Grand Staircase–Escalante National Monument and Dixie National Forest. Avoiding the interstate will add to your drive, but the scenery is well worth the extra time. SR 12 intersects with SR 24 in Torrey, which is just under 5 miles from the west side of Capitol Reef.

By air

Capitol Reef is 220 miles from Salt Lake City, and that is going to be your best option if you're not coming in from one of the other parks. There are small regional airports in the area as well, such as St. George Airport (SGU) near Zion, but they are not much closer to Capitol Reef and you will pay more to get there. Since you're probably combining a trip to Capitol Reef with visits to other parks, you might be flying in to Denver, Grand Junction, or Las Vegas. If so, be sure to check out our Suggested Itineraries section to learn how to best optimize your time.

CAPITOL REEF HIKING TRIPS

Capitol Reef offers adventure options for family members of all ages. Immediately off SR 24 are numerous short hikes that allow you to experience the history and ecology of the area. Farther south are several opportunities to get off the beaten path and explore less populated areas.

Petroglyph Walk

A very short walk along a boardwalk path that highlights the artwork of the ancient Fremont people.

Distance: 200 yards
Time: 10 minutes
Starting point: Pullout and parking lot just east of the visitor center on SR 24

A delightful and magical boardwalk runs through a shady cottonwood-tree grove along the base of the sandstone cliffs that hug SR 24 through the central part of Capitol Reef. Begin at the pullout and parking area where the obvious boardwalk is. Of the two boardwalks, the one on the left, which heads directly toward the cliff face, takes you to an educational sign and an audio recording by a modern-day Native American about the Fremont Indian petroglyphs. You will see a few glyphs ahead and up on the cliff.

Returning to the parking area, take the other boardwalk and follow it parallel to the base of the sandstone cliff. Keep a sharp eye on the cliff face, as there are multiple carving sites along the walk. You can get fairly close and take some nice photos.

Petroglyphs will likely inspire some imaginative stories from your kids. (NPS photo)

Small children and toddlers are safe to run back and forth on the boardwalk, and older children will enjoy a game of finding the hidden pictures.

Hickman Bridge

This short but popular hike to a beautiful arch, is very accessible, starting right from the main highway which runs through the park. The moderate elevation gain is not enough to worry about.

Distance: 1.8 miles roundtrip
Time: 1.5 hours
Starting point: The large parking area with bathrooms on SR 24 just east of the visitor center

Rangers tell us that this is the most popular hike in the park. It's just off the main road and about a mile each way to a beautiful arch (actually a natural bridge, formed by water) surrounded by impressive rock formations. It's definitely suitable for kids, even though it has a constant but moderate elevation gain. In fact, the hike has a pleasant variety of terrain, from modest scrambles around boulders to sandy washes, tight narrows, and slick rock faces, making it a moderate and interesting hike to a big payoff. Photographers will want to know that the light strikes the arch best for photos about one to one and a half hours after sunrise, but good luck getting your kids up that early!

Cohab Canyon

A moderate hike high above the canyon lets hikers experience the park from above. (Note that if you make this a 3.4-mile roundtrip, it's a more strenuous undertaking.)

Distance: 1.7 miles one way, with shuttle
Time: 1.5 to 2 hours
Starting point: Fruita Campground or SR 24 across from Petroglyph Walk

This hike is somewhat surprising in that it provides a wide variety of elements that make for a very pleasant outing. It's a point-to-point hike between the campground and the main road, and it's best to have someone shuttle the car, if possible, so you only have to do it in one direction. Regardless, we recommend starting at the north end of the trail and hiking toward the campground. If you don't have a shuttle but are doing the hike out and back, then definitely start from the north and hike until you get to the big overlook with views of the campground and old fruit orchards. From this point the trail drops steeply through a series of switchbacks exposed to the sun, so it would be a good spot to turn around and head back to your car.

The north end of the hike starts off in an area of black volcanic boulders that stand out in contrast to the other types of rock more common in southern Utah. This part of the trail is a bit uninspiring, but hang on, it gets better. As the trail moves farther away from the road, it enters a side canyon that has more

The character of the Cohab Canyon trail changes continually.

rewarding features. There are several pockets in the bottom of the wash that act as natural reservoirs for water, and some intriguing rock formations that resemble Swiss cheese. What could have caused those holes? As the trail continues the canyon narrows; it is in this area that our boys found small side canyons narrow enough in some places to be true slot canyons. We took the time to let them explore and climb in these spots, and we didn't mind doing so, because these areas tend to be cooler due to shade from the narrowly spaced walls.

When you reach the highest point of the trail, just before it drops to the campground, take a minute to marvel at the views. Then descend a series of switchbacks that drop quickly to the campground, or turn around and head back the way you came. Either way, this trail provides a nice quick outing for families, because features like the water pockets and slot canyons interest

Our boys love to explore slot canyons—we bet your kids will too.

kids, and remarkable geology and big views interest the adults. This makes for an enjoyable excursion for most any family.

Grand Wash

This is a bit longer hike than Cohab Canyon, but it has negligible elevation gain. It's hard to find shade for much of the trip, though the towering rock walls on either side may provide some respite from the sun at the right time of day. The scale of this canyon is huge!

Distance: 4.4 miles roundtrip
Time: 3 hours
Starting point: The east trailhead is on SR 24 in the parking area just 4.5 miles east of the visitor center. The west trailhead is on Scenic Drive about 3.5 miles south of the visitor center, by a large parking area with restrooms.

This hike takes you through a dry wash surrounded by towering cliffs, including a narrow section that resembles a slot canyon. It is one of the few ways to cross from one side of the Waterpocket Fold to the other, but you don't necessarily have to walk every bit of it. If you have someone to pick you up at the other end, you should plan this hike so that the sun is at your back.

One of the nice things about this hike is that in addition to the huge walls on either side of you, there are also some smaller side coves and hidden passages that kids love to explore. This is helpful because the sheer scale of your surroundings sometimes makes it feel as though you aren't making much progress. But toward the middle of the hike, the canyon narrows and the scale becomes more intimate (and the canyon shadier), which provides a pleasant change of pace and gives your kids more to experience up close and personally. The length and scale of this hike make it better suited to slightly older kids (ages eight or nine and up).

Side caves offer opportunity for exploration.

Cassidy Arch

A more strenuous hike that takes you high above the valley floor on a more technical trail. The arch itself is an attraction, but better still is the different vantage you get from climbing high up onto the top of the Waterpocket Fold.

Distance: 3.4 miles roundtrip, depending on starting and ending points
Time: 3 hours
Starting point: Trailhead is about 0.25 mile east of the western end of the Grand Wash Trail

This is a fairly strenuous hike with views of the surrounding canyons and a natural arch that is hidden from people on the canyon floor. You cannot see through the arch unless you get very close to it, so the experience is very different than the sort you would find at Arches National Park. Your path will take you

Some of the Cassidy Arch hike is along rugged trail.

over slickrock sandstone for the most part, and you will be hugging cliff sides and canyon rims where there are no guardrails for much of the trip, so think carefully before you bring young kids up here. Abby did this trail on her own last time around, but our nine- to thirteen-year-old boys could have done it. We recommend this as a morning hike; otherwise the afternoon sun will be on your back and hot for much of the hike. Bring plenty of water as there is none on this trail.

The trail begins inconspicuously off the north side of the Grand Wash Trail as you approach from the western end. It's easy to miss the trailhead the first time around because the large sign marking the trail is placed up a rise and is not obvious from the floor of the wash. You will see a sign reminding you to carry water; it's not only a good reminder but also a good landmark! When you see it, look up and follow what appears to be a social trail up a slickrock outcropping on the side of the wash. Once you do find the trail and start up it, you will see the sign that clearly marks your way.

This is the beginning of a long, uphill climb. You gain about 670 feet of elevation in the first mile, at which point the trail levels off for the most part and begin to follow the contours of the upper edges of the canyons. It is exhilarating to look down toward the canyon floor as you check your progress. At one point there is a very clear line of sight to the parking area and outhouses below. If you've left family members there, it's fun to yell down to them and imagine the surprise on their faces as they see how far up you are.

The trail's serpentine route leads to canyons tucked away behind the main canyon you left. Around each bend you will be tempted to look around for the arch—it's surprising how many corners have to be turned until it finally appears across a chasm!

That's right, you won't get a chance to get all that close to Cassidy Arch. The views of this feature are from across a chasm. Although it's beautiful, it seems more like you have discovered a hidden treasure than hiked to a specific destination. In fact, it's difficult to ascertain where the end of the actual trail is. If

Cassidy Arch hangs high above the canyon floor.

you hike until you see the arch, you've accomplished your goal and can turn around at any point to return to the canyon floor the way you came. However, if at this point you are still up for some hiking and you feel confident in your ability to routefind across slickrock, you can continue in a southwest direction, continually angling toward the arch. The trail can be faint at best, so keep a lookout for cairns. Eventually, you will reach the arch. It's well worth the added effort; think Delicate Arch but without the crowds!

Overall, the feeling of accomplishment from having climbed a difficult trail, the exhilaration of finding yourselves on the top of the canyon walls, and the hidden treasure of Cassidy Arch are all great rewards for the hard work this trip requires.

On a side note, if you're in very good shape and have someone to drop you off and shuttle your car back to the campgrounds, you can actually continue your hike from the Cassidy Arch Trail along the Frying Pan Trail to where it joins the Cohab

Canyon Trail and eventually into camp. It's a good idea to talk to a ranger ahead of time for a trail of this length and difficulty to make sure your party is well prepared.

Headquarters Canyon

Headquarters Canyon (in the southern section of Capitol Reef) is a primitive but easy trail that calls for some routefinding and takes you into a slot canyon inside the Waterpocket Fold. Hiking in this part of the park requires a bit of a time commitment because the drive into this region is via a long gravel road, sometimes in poor condition, far from the more populated areas of the park.

Distance: 2 miles roundtrip
Time estimate: 1.5–2 hours
Starting point: To access any of these small canyons, you will take the Notom–Bullfrog Road (located to the east of the main visitor center area) south from SR 24. Stop at the visitor center first to check on road conditions, as this road is sometimes washed out, full of washboarded sections, or worse.

Even a sign as big as this one can be easy to miss.

Along the Notom–Bullfrog Road you encounter a fork. Stay left (turning right would take you up Burr Trail Road toward Boulder). In just under 2.5 miles you reach an intersection. The right-hand turn leads to what is known as the Post Corral. A pullout area at this junction, on the east side, is your best bet for parking. If cars are already there, you can head all the way down to the old corral and park there (it's 0.5 mile back to the trailhead from here). Note: there is a pit toilet at the Post Corral.

One prominent website we used to plan our trip said that the trail leaves from the old corral. We did this but ended up at a much shorter and less well-known canyon. If you want to hike to Headquarters Canyon, you need to leave from the trailhead sign at the junction.

Although many unnamed canyons cut into the eastern side of the Waterpocket Fold, Headquarters Canyon is one of the better-known, and therefore named, slot canyons here. It's a good option if you feel like getting off the beaten path and seeing another part of the park. Most of these slot canyons don't cut very deeply into the fold, and many trails into them are blocked by pools of standing water for most of the year (read more on these below). Headquarters Canyon is always accessible except after heavy rain. It's not a difficult hike but does take some navigation skills. It's seldom traveled and not well marked. Hikers need to be willing to do some routefinding using rock cairns and feel comfortable not always being sure they're on the right path. That said, it is extremely difficult to get lost entirely, since the Waterpocket Fold provides a mountainous landmark with which to keep your bearings.

Once you locate the trailhead sign, head past it toward the Waterpocket Fold. A huge red sandstone outcropping, roughly triangular in shape, is a good landmark here. Walk toward it. You will skirt around it to the left when you reach it. There is a bit of a trail as you head across the flat ground, but it is very primitive.

This primitive trail leads toward the triangular rock outcropping.

That landmark rock—you're on the right track!

If you lose sight of the trail at any point, head toward the left-hand side of the triangular rock outcropping. Once you reach it head to the left side, but be careful! You do *not* want to take the trail that hugs the rock. Rocks may be placed across that trail to deter you, but they can be easy to miss. When you reach the left side of the red boulder, go left away from it on the trail heading that direction.

Just after skirting the rock and bending left away from it, look for a dry streambed; you should see rock cairns marking the way. From here you basically follow the dry riverbed. At times you leave the river to go around an obstacle, but return to it shortly. Be very careful at these junctions, as the trail sometimes crosses the river instead of following it. Look all around you at each junction of river and trail to determine if you should join the riverbed or cross from one side to the other. When we went, there were rocks placed across the way if you were not to leave

Heading into the slot section

or enter the riverbed. Overall, the path is fairly clear if you take your time, making sure to follow the cairns and watching for stones laid across the trail to turn you away.

As the trail winds in and out of the riverbed, you hike over a few humps and do a bit of rock scrambling. Keep your eyes open for wildlife along here. We had fun watching a fearless jackrabbit hop down the trail ahead of us! Eventually the riverbed clearly leads you toward an opening in the Waterpocket Fold. The cliffs tower over you, and a crack opens up before you. Although the hike has been pleasant until now (and our kids loved being routefinders), here is where it really gets fun.

Once in the slot, you can't go wrong. Parents, relax and let the kids climb, run, and explore. Although it's called a slot canyon, it's really only narrow in the beginning section.

Past the first part, the canyon opens up a bit. The canyon walls still soar above you, but there is a bit more space on the ground. You can hike in as far as you like. Eventually you reach a dry-fall, a pile of boulders blocking your way. Turn and head back or try to find a route around them. For most of us, this is the turnaround point.

Head back the way you came, still vigilant for the rock cairns to make sure you're headed in the right direction. Look for the landmark rock marking your way and hike back across the flat grass and scrubland to your car.

A note about the other canyons in this area: a number of other cracks lead back into the Waterpocket Fold. We found some to the south of Headquarters Canyon, and Surprise Canyon is just to the north. While you're in this part of the park, consider whether your family would find it fun to explore more. We had some lovely hikes along dry riverbeds, venturing into some smaller canyons and climbing around near hidden pools of water. Just park and hike off toward the Waterpocket Fold. Keep your eyes open for cracks or openings in the cliff walls and head toward them. If you're relaxed about your time and not too concerned with any specific destination, you can find some beautiful and remote places to explore down in this end of the park!

OTHER ACTIVITIES IN CAPITOL REEF

In case you're looking for something more, here are a few other options, besides hiking, for enjoying Capitol Reef.

Wildlife viewing

Because Capitol Reef's visitor center lies along a creek with year-round water that supports an orchard and a green riparian area of substantial size, it's one of the few parks in southern

These bighorn sheep ewes call Capitol Reef home.

Utah where you have a decent chance of spotting some larger animals. During our time there we saw deer, wild turkey, and bighorn sheep, all right from the road or in the campground. As usual, early morning and early evening are the best times to spot wildlife, especially during the warmer months.

Bicycling

Bicycling is allowed only on paved roads open to vehicle traffic. Since these roads have a lot of turns, very little shoulder, and many motorists paying closer attention to the scenery than to their driving, we would suggest that cycling in Capitol Reef with your kids is not a great option.

Canyoneering

There are not a lot of options for canyoneering here, especially in the main portions of the park. However, one of the better-known slot canyons in the region, Headquarters Canyon, is in the more remote southeast portion of Capitol Reef. See the Capitol Reef Hiking Trips section above.

Backpacking

Capitol Reef offers a number of backcountry backpacking options, particularly in the southern portion of the park. These trails are rugged, the weather is warm, and water is scarce. For these reasons, we don't feel the backpacking options here are really suitable for younger kids, but if you have teens anxious for a wilderness experience, you can find more information about backcountry options on the park's website. If you plan on camping overnight, pick up free but required permits at the visitor center.

CAPITOL REEF CAMPING AND LODGING

There is no lodge in Capitol Reef, and there are only three campgrounds. One is large and well developed, and the other two are remote and primitive.

The immensity of the desert can give you a new perspective.

Fruita Campground

The feel of this campground is different from any other we've stayed in when visiting Utah because it's in the orchard of an old farmstead that makes up Capitol Reef's headquarters area. There is soft grass, and large trees provide ample shade and ideal spots to hang a hammock. Because this area is so lush, the wildlife is quite abundant, and you're almost sure to see deer and wild turkeys. In fact, we were asked to take down our hammocks in the evenings, as startled deer have been known to crash into them when they're strung between trees! From this campground it's a short walk to the Gifford House, where some of our fondest memories are of sinking our teeth into those pies after a week of camp-cooked meals. Capitol Reef is unique in that the human history of the area is highlighted almost as much as the natural history, and the beauty and comfort of the campground reflect that. If you're fortunate enough to be there in the fall, you're actually free to take advantage of the fruit trees by picking some choice specimens to nourish you on your trip.

The campground spots are first come, first served, so it pays to get there as early as possible. If you feel you need reservations, there are several hotels just west of the park in the town of Torrey.

Cedar Mesa Campground

This is an undeveloped and unmonitored campground on Notom–Bullfrog Road, which goes down the eastern side of the park into more primitive areas. This could possibly be considered a "last-resort" camping area, as it has only five or six sites with a pit toilet and no water. It's first come, first served, and it's on a small rise in thick brush that does provide a degree of shade. The road leading to it is gravel with washboard ruts and some creek crossings, so we're serious when we say it's more primitive. However, the creek crossings are really nothing more than sandy washes, so as long as the weather is dry, most any vehicle can handle this road. Just be aware that you're going to get rattled a bit by the washboarding.

Cathedral Valley Campground

Similar to Cedar Mesa Campground, Cathedral Valley Campground has only five or six sites with a pit toilet and no water, and it is first come, first served. It's 36 miles from the visitor center in the remote Cathedral Valley area. Due to the ruggedness of this part of the park, we don't consider it a possibility for most families. Because most family-friendly hikes are in the central and southern parts of the park, this campground would not be an ideal base.

BRYCE CANYON NATIONAL PARK

Bryce Canyon is a splash of color and bizarre shapes that creates one of the most unusual landscapes we've ever encountered, and once again we found ourselves in a national park quite unlike any other. Despite its close proximity to Zion and Capitol Reef, Bryce is nothing like either of them. Some things that set Bryce apart: hoodoos, high elevation, distance from towns and cities, and a wide variety of ecosystems near each other. Bryce's hiking opportunities have a flavor all their own, and it boasts the best air quality of all the parks, which contributes to dark night skies perfect for stargazing. Yet these are just a few of the qualities that make Bryce Canyon National Park special.

Bryce Canyon became a national park in 1928, named for Mormon pioneer and early settler Ebenezer Bryce. Although it's called a canyon, it is not a canyon in the true sense of the word. Canyons are carved by the eroding action of a river, whereas Bryce Canyon is formed by the freeze-thaw cycle of precipitated water. In the case of the hoodoos in Bryce, the limestone Claron Formation is softer than the layer above it. As the water from rain and snow seeps down into this softer layer and then freezes, it creates tremendous pressure that eventually breaks off large chunks of rock. As these pieces of rock break off, tall fins or slender hoodoos are left behind. A hoodoo is shaped through a series of erosions: first a fin is formed, then a window opens up in the fin, and then the window expands to an arch, which eventually breaks down into two hoodoos. If you're interested in learning more about the unique geology of this park, you will find plenty to whet your appetite in the visitor center and other displays around the park.

112   UTAH'S BIG FIVE NATIONAL PARKS

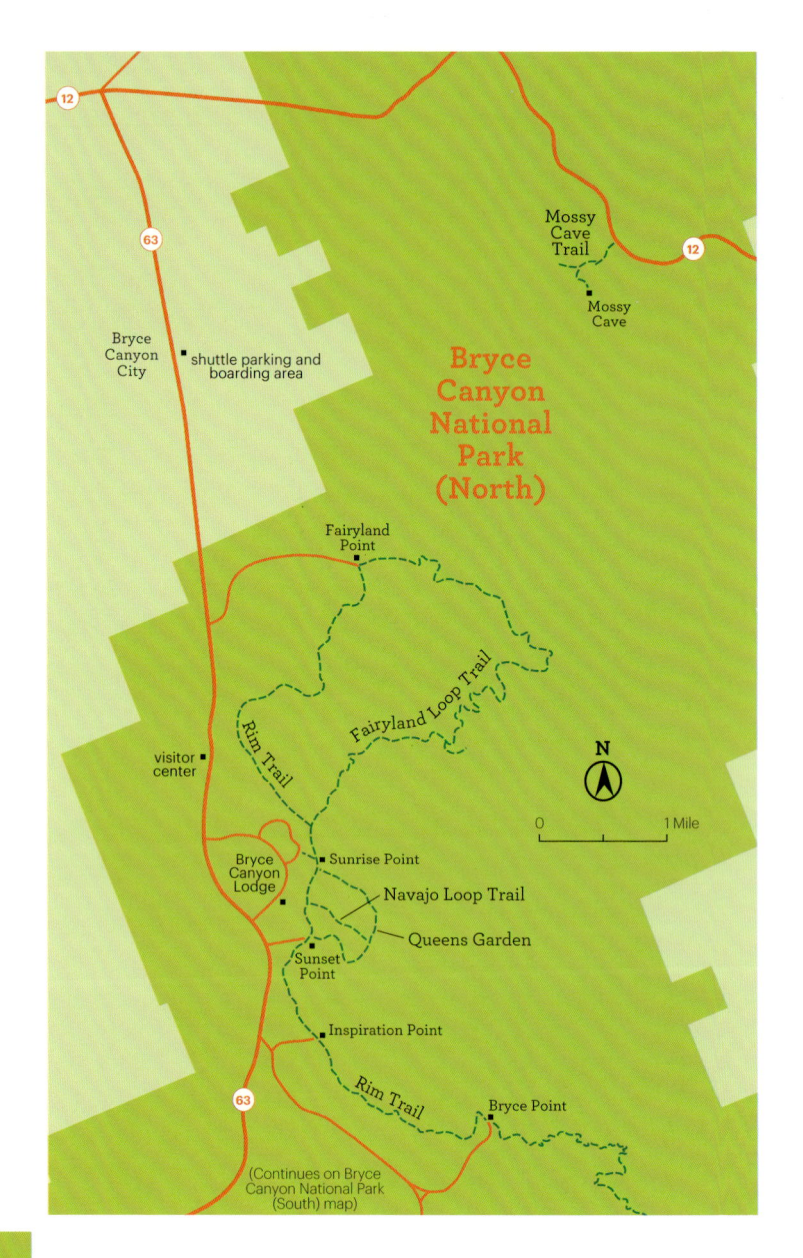

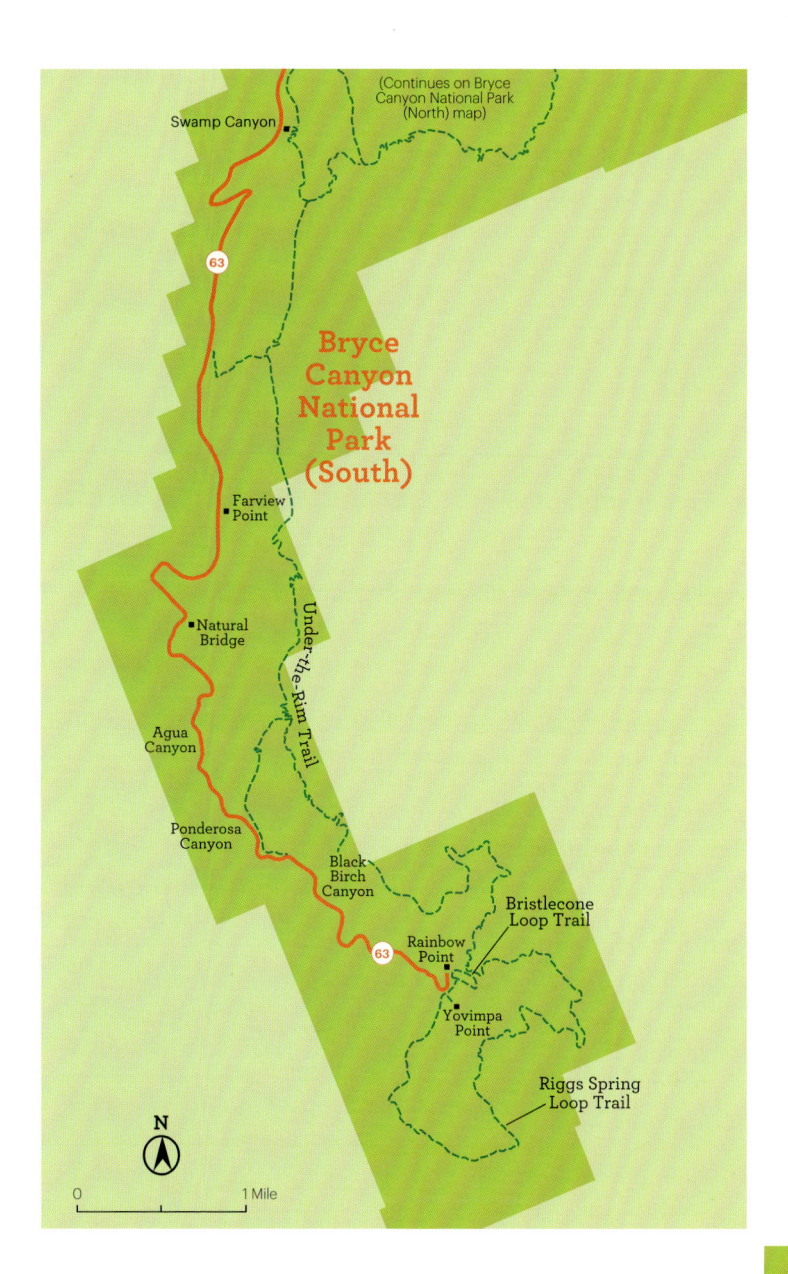

BRYCE CANYON NATIONAL PARK 113

Bryce Canyon National Park is immense.

Bryce Canyon is a long, narrow park stretching from north to south with the main entrance and visitor center at the northern end. Most of the major hiking trails are in the northern section of the park. A long scenic drive follows the canyon rim nearly to the park's southern end, and there are many stops along this drive for viewing the changing character of the canyon. A parking area at the end launches backpackers onto some of the main backcountry trails but also includes a good shorter hike for families. The park slowly rises in elevation as you move from north to south, with the elevation at the road's southern terminus, Rainbow Point, coming in at 9115 feet! Due to the high elevation, you may experience difficulty breathing, light-headedness, and perhaps a feeling of being a bit "off" when you're hiking in this area. Take your time, rest as often as anyone in your group needs it, and make sure everyone drinks a lot of water!

In an effort to preserve the good air quality and also to alleviate parking problems, Bryce Canyon National Park offers a free shuttle service roughly from early May to early October. If you're staying outside the park, you can leave your car at Ruby's Inn, just outside the main entrance, to help reduce parking issues in the park. The bus makes frequent regularly scheduled stops throughout the day at all the main areas of interest in the upper portion of the park. Two scheduled tours per day take visitors all the way to Rainbow Point. These free tours require advance registration at the visitor center. You can find more information and printed schedules online as well as at the visitor center. The shuttle is not mandatory, but visitors are encouraged to use it as much as possible since it helps maintain the park environment and improve the experience for all.

Read the National Park Service's two main publications for visitors: the one-page park guide and the very helpful park newspaper, which has detailed information about hiking trails, current programs, safety alerts, and more. Some parks will give you both publications upon entry, but we had to ask for the newspaper at Bryce. If they don't hand it to you at the entry gate, ask for it.

GETTING TO BRYCE CANYON

Whether you travel to Utah by air or by car, you will have to drive to actually visit the park unless you come by tour bus.

A natural bridge overlook en route to Rainbow Point

By car

From the north (Salt Lake City) take I-15 south to exit 95 and drive east on State Route 20 to US Highway 89 south. From US 89, go east on SR 12 to SR 63. SR 63 will take you south into Bryce Canyon National Park.

From Zion National Park, follow SR 9 east to US 89. Travel north on US 89 to SR 12 and follow directions above.

From Capitol Reef National Park, head west on SR 24 to SR 12. Go south on SR 12 to reach SR 63.

By air

Bryce is 270 miles from Las Vegas (LAS) and Salt Lake City (SLC). Smaller regional airports include Saint George, Utah (SGU), 49 miles away; and Cedar City, Utah (CDC), 60 miles away.

BRYCE CANYON HIKING TRIPS

The hikes in Bryce Canyon can be divided into two categories: those on the rim of the canyon and those that take you down into the canyon and hoodoos. The rugged and colorful hoodoos are so vast and expansive that making the effort to see them from varied perspectives is well worth the effort.

Sunset Point to Sunrise Point

If you have time to get out of the car only once, this is the place to do it. This isn't so much a hike as a stroll along a paved path adjacent to parking lots in many spots, but it will showcase the best views the park has to offer.

Distance: 1 mile roundtrip
Time: 1–1.5 hours
Starting point: Sunset Point

This trail is a mostly level, paved walk along the upper rim of Bryce Canyon. It offers good views of the hoodoos from above, it's wheelchair accessible, and pets are allowed. The return trail is along the same path.

If you prefer to do this in only one direction, the shuttle bus picks up and drops off at both Sunrise and Sunset points. Both of the park's campgrounds are near the two endpoints, so if you would like to add distance to your hike and you're staying in one of the campgrounds, you could hike from your camp. This section of trail is also part of the longer Rim Trail. Finally, if you haven't guessed from the names, the start and end points are great places to take photographs at sunrise and sunset. You might plan your hike around one of those times of day to get the best photo ops. If those are hard times to get your family on the trail, as they are for us, both points are near the campgrounds and have large parking areas, so a quick trip over just for photos while the kids are still in their sleeping bags is an option too.

Bryce Amphitheatre

Rim Trail

This trail follows the edge of the canyon and visits all of the best overlooks. It spans 5.5 miles in its entirety, so you can pick and choose which sections you want to tackle. If you would rather leave the rim and drop into the canyon to see hoodoos up close, skip to the next section of trails, like Queens Garden and Navajo Loop.

Distance: 2–11 miles, roundtrip
Time: Depends on the distance you choose
Starting point: Many locations along the rim of the canyon, including (from north to south) Fairyland Point, North Campground, Sunrise Point, Sunset Point, Inspiration Point, and Bryce Point; all but Fairyland Point are shuttle stops.

The Rim Trail gives you many opportunities to view hoodoos and the character of the canyon from above and is on the list of hikes to choose from to accomplish the "I Hiked the Hoodoos!" program. The trail is all hard-packed dirt and gravel except between Sunrise and Sunset points, where it's paved.

We hiked various sections of this trail as a family, but we also dropped Harley at Fairyland Point and he hiked back to North Campground, where we were staying. The kids climbed and played all over by the trail as it came through camp while they waited for Dad to get back. The following chart gives the distances between points. Distances are one-way and are cumulative since the trail is one long line.

Distances along Rim Trail	
Fairyland Point to Sunrise Point	2.5 miles
Sunrise Point to Sunset Point	0.5 mile
Sunset Point to Inspiration Point	0.7 mile
Inspiration Point to Bryce Point	1.5 miles

There really isn't a bad section of this trail because it simply follows the edge of the rim around Bryce Amphitheater, the park's main attraction. Our family walked the most popular section between Sunrise and Sunset points but spent most of our time on the trails below the rim, getting closer views of the hoodoos. If you want to get away from the crowds and enjoy the amazing scenery with a little less hustle and bustle, hike the trail from Fairyland Point south to Sunset Point or the North Campground. That section follows the rim of neighboring Campbell Canyon, basically a slightly smaller version of Bryce, with all the same colors and strange formations on a slightly less spectacular but still amazing scale. It is not a must-do if you're pressed for time, but if you want to stretch your legs a bit and can't get enough of those orange and pink rocks, it's a way to do it and enjoy a bit more solitude. Because the shuttle doesn't make it out to Fairyland Point (thus the smaller crowds), you'll need to arrange your own transportation if you want to do that section.

Queens Garden

This ranks as our favorite hike in the park. To get the most of it, start at either Sunrise or Sunset Point and include either half of the Navajo Loop as well as the Queens Garden Trail. This will add up to just under 3 miles total and will show you the best the park has to offer from a number of different vantage points, both above and below the rim. We describe it in a clockwise direction, which means a steep climb at the end, but either direction works. A classic.

Entering the trees on the Queens Garden hike

Sure, you can hike through walls!

Distance: 1.8 miles roundtrip to Queens Garden; about 3 miles with Navajo Loop
Time: 1–2 hours
Starting point: Sunrise Point

The Queens Garden Trail is the least difficult descent into the hoodoos. It has an elevation loss and gain of about 357 feet; remember that whatever you hike down into, you will have to hike back out of again! The Queens Garden is part of the "I Hiked the Hoodoos!" program, and it's named for the views it gives of

"Queen Victoria," one of the named hoodoos. The best view of her is from a spur trail. The Queens Garden Trail can also be combined with the Navajo Loop if you're up for a bit more of a climb on the way out.

This trail is a must as long as everyone in your family is up for a little bit of moderate hiking. The Queens Garden hike takes you immediately down into the hoodoos. Your kids will be so fascinated by what they're seeing that they will likely forget that they're burning calories. You head downhill for much of the hike as you pass through a forest of hoodoo spires. At one point you get to walk through a window in a fin that our kids enjoyed tremendously (maybe it was jumping out on the other side and scaring Abby that they enjoyed . . . hard to tell!).

Whenever you feel tired and need to head back, you can just return the way you came. Once you get to the spur trail to see Queen Victoria, you're about halfway to the Navajo Loop Trail. The trail also gets much more level at this point, and you enter the trees for a bit and get some shade.

When you reach the Navajo Loop Trail (branching off to the left and right), decide whether you will turn around and head back the way you came or continue on and join the Navajo Loop, which has new and equally incredible sights. Some things to consider when making this decision: If you join the Navajo Loop, you will only complete half of the loop and you will have to decide whether to head right or left along the loop. Either way it's about 0.6 mile from here to the loop's endpoint, Sunset Point, but both sides climb very steeply as they ascend from the canyon bottom. It's farther, distance-wise, to go back along Queens Garden, but the incline is more moderate. If you're hiking on a hot day, the Navajo Loop offers more shade and can actually be quite cool in areas.

In order to decide, read up on both hikes and then be prepared to see how your family is doing when you reach this junction point. Flexibility is key at times like these.

Navajo Loop Trail

Another great trail for dropping below the rim and getting in among the hoodoos, this one has a pretty steep switchback section that is well maintained but will get you breathing hard. We love to combine this trail with the Queens Garden Trail for an awesome loop of just under 3 miles.

Distance: 1.3-mile loop (3 miles with Queens Garden)
Time: 1.5 hours
Starting point: Sunset Point

The wonderful Navajo Loop Trail descends via a long, steep set of constructed stone switchbacks akin to an ancient, cobbled Roman road. The elevation loss, then gain, of this loop is 550 feet, most of it at the beginning and end of the hike. Once you drop down off this steep portion of the trail, you enter a forest made up of trees and hoodoo spires. The burnt umber color of the stone mixed with the deep green of the pine trees makes for a beautiful hiking experience. If at all possible, take your family into this wonderland! The trail gives you views of the famous park landmarks Thor's Hammer, Wall Street, and Two Bridges. It's also a hike on the list for completing "I Hiked the Hoodoos!"

As you hike up out of the Navajo Loop, you pass some cool natural bridges. A bridge is different from an arch because it is formed by a river or stream that flows under it. Find these bridges by looking up into a few of the crevices along the way—there's even a double bridge!

A note about joining the Navajo Loop with the Queens Garden: As we pointed out above, you will have to decide whether to hike these two trails separately or together. We recommend that you hike them together, assuming each member of your family is able. If you do only one of them, do the Queens Garden. If you make it all the way to the turnaround point on that trail, it's actually shorter to continue on to the Navajo Loop than to turn around and go back. This does result in a steeper climb out of the canyon, but we found that allowing each person to make the climb at their own speed meant we could all complete the hike. If you plan to do both trails, there's not much point to doing them separately, except that if you do them jointly, you will miss out on half of the Navajo Loop. With so many things to see and limited time, we found that hiking them in a single outing allowed for the best views of the most scenery in the least time and with the least effort.

Finally, we must include a discussion about which direction to go. The park newspaper suggests going clockwise (from Sunrise Point/Queens Garden to Sunset Point/Navajo Loop). This was what we had seen recommended in various places online, and it was what we planned to do. Once we got there, many people recommended the opposite direction. We weren't sure what to do but stuck with our original plan and were glad we did. Going clockwise (Sunrise to Sunset) means you will have a more gradual descent and a steeper ascent. Obviously,

Down among the hoodoos

reversing the direction switches that. You will need to think about which would be better for your family, and also take into consideration the time of day and the expected temperatures and sun exposure. We were happy with the clockwise direction on a day with moderate temperatures, so that's our recommendation under these conditions.

Remember that whichever direction you go, you will not be coming out of the canyon at the same place you started. It's a 0.5-mile hike along a paved portion of the Rim Trail (see Sunset Point to Sunrise Point hike) to return to your parked car. You can also ride the shuttle between the two, but we found the wait for the shuttle longer than just walking back. You could also send an adult family member back to bring the car around.

Bristlecone Loop

This is a short loop at the south end of the road and the highest point in the park. It provides a different perspective due to the different forest at this elevation and the views of the surrounding region that spread to the south. The drive to the southern tip of the park takes quite a bit of time, but if you're taking the time to visit this portion of the park, adding forty-five minutes to an hour for this hike is worth it.

Distance: 1-mile loop
Time: 1 hour
Starting point: Rainbow Point, southern end of the park

Bristlecone Loop is a delightful change from the desert hikes in Bryce Canyon. It's easily doable by all and is a great opportunity to see a part of the park that's a bit different from the upper section. It's a hike on the "I Hiked the Hoodoos!" list, and its elevation changes by only 200 feet. However, it's the highest hike in the park, meaning you will experience the effects of thinner air here more than anywhere else. Stay hydrated and rest as often as needed! Remember, you can drive down to this part of the park (a 40-mile roundtrip), but you could also take the shuttle and save your gas. Make sure you tell the rangers when you sign up for the shuttle that you want to hike the Bristlecone Loop while at Rainbow Point. They will tell you if you have time or if you need to return on the later bus.

The trail starts from a large parking area with outhouse toilets and picnic areas. Find the trailhead and walk into a unique ecosystem of old-growth bristlecone pines and spruce-fir forests. The path is hard dirt in some places and gravel in others but always level and easy to walk. We were all interested in interpretive signs along the way telling about the bristlecone pine; some of the cones are more than 1800 years old. One of our boys said, "Have I ever seen anything that old?!"

Lacking much undergrowth, the mature forest in this area might seem an environment without wildlife; but, in fact, it's the perfect place for certain animals to flourish. Expect to see Steller's jays and ravens in abundance. This is also good habitat

Photos confirm that you've "hiked the hoodoos."

BRYCE CANYON NATIONAL PARK 127

for grouse, woodpeckers, owls, squirrels, and chipmunks. All of these creatures may show themselves if you find a quiet place to sit and be still. There is a wonderful spot to do just that when you reach a small covered shelter and some benches. From here, views reach as far as the Four Corners and into all the surrounding areas as you sit above the canyon. After a rest to take in the wildlife and views, continue around the loop to the parking area.

Keep in mind that the drive down here might take longer than expected and that you may want to stop to view the many features along the way. Visiting this end of the park can easily take up your whole day!

Mossy Cave

Still in Bryce Canyon National Park, but not in the main part of the park so you don't have to pay to access this hike. The trailhead is along SR 12 east of the main park turnoff.

Distance: 0.8 mile roundtrip
Time: 1 hour due to viewing opportunities
Starting point: Parking area off SR 12 to the north and east of the park. (Note: This is outside the main park. There is no entrance fee for this hike.)

A mossy, wet cave and a waterfall contribute to making this a fun hike. The trail is part of the "I Hiked the Hoodoos!" program, and it's fairly easy but does include a 200-foot elevation gain that may get you winded. It's mostly hard-packed dirt with some areas of loose gravel. There are many "social" trails in the waterfall area, making it hard to know which one to follow. (A social trail is an unofficial trail made by people leaving the main trail, usually as a shortcut or to a different view of some feature. They are not a good thing, as they often damage sensitive areas and cause erosion. You can avoid contributing to this kind of damage by keeping your kids on the main, marked trails.) The

National Park Service has not marked the official trail well, but it's hard to get lost. Most of the social trails will lead you to the waterfall, and one social trail leads across the stream above the waterfall and up the steep side of a ridge toward a window or arch in the wall at the top. That is a dangerous and prohibited route, but many people do it anyway; we helped rescue a woman who had fallen and broken her ankle on the way down from there! Please stay off the social trails. The official trail ends at the waterfall.

As you leave the parking lot you hike along a "stream" that was once part of an old irrigation ditch, the Tropic Ditch. The color of the rocks and the clarity of the water are phenomenal here. You begin to climb a bit and are forced to choose a direction at a fork in the trail. The left side takes you on a

The viewing area for Mossy Cave

short spur trail to Mossy Cave, and the right side leads to the waterfall.

The trail to Mossy Cave becomes much steeper. You enter forested terrain (a nice shade break on a hot day!) that stays with you until you reach the cave. The cave itself is a bit of a letdown. You cannot go in the cave ("boo" say our kids) but there is an interpretive sign discussing the importance of seep areas like this to the wildlife and plant communities in the vicinity. The cave is pretty, and it's remarkable how much cooler the air immediately outside the cave is, but overall we were a bit disappointed with Mossy Cave.

Staying to the right at the fork will take you to the waterfall. The trail leads to the top of the falls, where the view of them is not too good. You will see better views of the falls as you climb toward them, so get your pictures on the way up!

While there were good parts of this hike, it's probably not worth a special trip if you're mostly in the main part of the park or if you come to the park from the west. If, however, you're approaching the park from the east on SR 12, you might consider including it as a short stop. And if you're here in the fall, the foliage colors along here are the best in the park!

Other Hiking Options Inside Bryce Canyon Amphitheater

The following two trails are very popular but not very appropriate for most families. While we didn't personally try them, we would be remiss if we didn't mention them. If your family is up for the challenge of these longer, more strenuous hikes, you can find more information online at the National Park Service site or with a Google search.

Fairyland Loop

We decided against doing this well-known hike that crosses some beautiful areas north of the main amphitheater because it is 8 miles long and rated as strenuous. If you have older kids who are go-getters, however, you should consider it.

Distance: 8 miles
Time: 4–5 hours
Starting point: Fairyland Point or north of Sunrise Point

The less crowded Fairyland Loop trail has an elevation change of 1716 feet and takes you past the China Wall, Tower Bridge, and many other tall hoodoos.

Peek-A-Boo Loop

Peek-A-Boo Loop is a long and strenuous hike through the heart of Bryce Amphitheater.

Distance: 5.5 miles
Time: 3–4 hours
Starting point: Bryce Point

A steep but spectacular hike that takes you to the Wall of Windows and away from the crowds. You can also save your legs and go on a guided horseback ride instead.

OTHER ACTIVITIES IN BRYCE CANYON

Wildlife viewing

Although there are various types of wildlife in the area, the terrain naturally concentrates the visitors in certain places, pushing much of the wildlife into other regions. You have ample opportunity to view Utah prairie dogs between the front gate and the visitor center; signs point out where the colonies live. They were listed as an endangered species in 1973 but upgraded to a threatened species in 1994 due to preservation and protection efforts. Various ranger programs are devoted to teaching about these prairie dogs and finding opportunities to view them. Check the listing of ranger programs in the visitor center for the most up-to-date information. Other wildlife species in the park that are protected under the Endangered Species Act are the California condor and the southwestern willow flycatcher.

You may also have the chance to see Steller's jays (check out the Bristlecone Loop hike), Great Basin rattlesnakes, golden-mantled ground squirrels, pronghorns (sometimes called antelope), chipmunks, mountain lions, violet-green swallows, and Clark's nutcrackers, to name a few. For the most part, the rattlesnakes and mountain lions are reclusive and avoid areas that have a lot of people. No special precautions are recommended other than staying alert to your surroundings. Camping is a great way to have plenty of time to sit quietly, relax, and watch for animal visitors to pass by. Otherwise, backpacking to less busy areas might be an option for your family. See Backpacking below.

Horseback riding

A great way to view the hoodoos in Bryce Canyon is by horseback. Canyon Trail Rides offers two- and four-hour horse and mule rides into the Bryce Amphitheater on a dedicated horse trail and on the Peek-A-Boo Loop Trail. If you think you would like to give riding a try, check out their website (see Resources).

Backpacking

The backpacking opportunities in Bryce are slightly limited largely due to the smaller size of the park. The main trails are Under-the-Rim and the Riggs Spring Loop trails. Both have backcountry campsites. Both lead below the rim of the canyon and through forested areas. A permit is required for all backcountry camping and hiking. Permits are issued by a ranger at the visitor center and costs vary, depending on the number of campers. You can make a reservation in person up to 48 hours in advance of your trip. You must also pick up your permit in person from the visitor center from 8:00 AM to one hour before close. Although the chances of seeing a bear are low, the NPS is requiring the use of bear canisters in the backcountry. You can bring your own or borrow (free of charge) one from the visitor center. If you plan on backcountry hiking and camping, make sure you understand all the backcountry information on the park's website.

Riggs Spring Loop is a 9-mile loop. The Under-the-Rim Trail extends for 23 miles from Bryce Point to Rainbow Point. Remember that a shuttle runs along the canyon, and backpackers may use it to connect the ends of the Under-the-Rim Trail or to limit the number of cars parked in the Rainbow Point parking area.

BRYCE CANYON CAMPING AND LODGING

Bryce National Park has two options for overnight guests who don't plan on staying in the backcountry. The first is Bryce Canyon Lodge. The other option is to camp in one of its two developed campgrounds.

The Lodge

Bryce Canyon Lodge is between Sunrise and Sunset points. It's one of the grand western lodges built for the National Park System in the 1920s, and it retains its rustic elegance amid the modern world—it's well worth a visit. It's part of a large complex of buildings that includes a laundry and pay showers. Some of the ranger programs, including nighttime astronomy programs, are held in meeting rooms at the lodge. If you're coming to the lodge for a program, leave time to find the right place, as the building complex is large and can be confusing.

The lodge, operated by Forever Resorts, boasts 114 rooms comprising lodge suites, hotel rooms, and cabins. The dining room is open for breakfast, lunch, and dinner (reservations recommended). You can reserve your room over the phone or online—see Resources. Note: None of the rooms or lobby areas has a television.

Campgrounds

There are two developed campgrounds in the park: North Campground and Sunset Campground, each located centrally near the main hiking areas and the lodge with its coin-operated laundry and shower facilities (open only in the summer months).

Both campgrounds have flush toilets and drinking water. There are no RV hook-ups, but there is a fee-for-use dump station at the south end of North Campground (also summer only). Both campgrounds have sites available to reserve ahead of time and some that are first come, first served only. All sites usually fill by afternoon during the summer months.

North Campground

This large campground is in a ponderosa-pine forest with areas of shade and sun. It's nestled up against the Rim Trail, with some sites directly adjacent to the trail and nearest to the General Store. It has thirteen RV sites (no hook-ups) available by advance reservation and eighty-six RV and tent sites available on a first come, first served basis. The roads in and around the camp area can be a bit confusing at times, so take care not to get lost! You can make reservations for one of the RV sites ahead of time. Loops A and B are for RVs, and Loops C and D are for tent campers. At least one loop is open year-round. We found the North Campground sites to be pleasant but without much privacy.

Sunset Campground

Sunset Campground is slightly smaller than North Campground, with about one hundred total sites in three loops. Unlike North Campground, it has twenty tent campsites that can be reserved ahead of time. Loop A is for RV campers, and Loops B and C are for tent campers. This campground is west of Sunset Point and approximately 1.5 miles south of the visitor center in a ponderosa-pine forest with a mix of sun and shade.

One final note about camping options: we were worried we might not get one of the first come, first served campsites when we visited recently. Our backup plan was to check and see if the Yovimpa Pass backcountry campsite was available. It's only 1.6 miles down the Riggs Spring Loop Trail, with minimal elevation change. We thought we could probably get all the things we actually needed down to the campsite in a few trips. It wouldn't be ideal, but it'd be better than being turned away entirely if the main campground was full. Keep this in mind if your family or group is hardy and strong. Also keep in mind you will be camping at around 9000 feet if you choose this option, so make sure you're prepared for cold backcountry situations.

A typical campsite in the North Campground

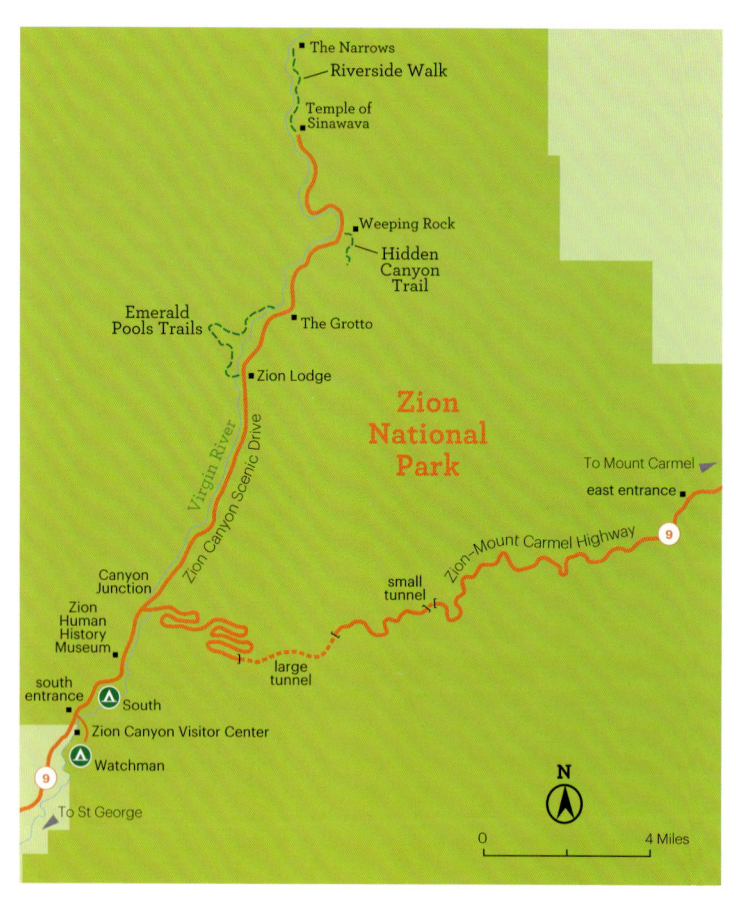

If you would like more detail, online versions of this map, which allow the user to zoom in and out, are available at the National Park Service's website for Zion.

ZION NATIONAL PARK

For us, Zion National Park was something quite unexpected! From the moment we entered through the incredible tunnel by the east entrance until the moment we left out the west side, we were awed and amazed. Although the part of the park that sees the majority of visitors is one big gorge, there is so much to see and do in that single area. Of course, we also visited some paths less traveled throughout the park, but there's enough to capture your imagination in just the main Zion Canyon. In addition to the hikes and activities we will share with you, there are a few things you should know before you go.

First, because so many visitors journey to Zion each year (more than three million in 2014) and because they are geographically concentrated, the National Park Service has instituted a mandatory shuttle system through the main canyon. Before we went, we weren't sure how we felt about this. We kind of like our freedom, and we like to have our huge car full of all of our stuff right at hand. Once we were there and ready to explore, we reluctantly boarded and hoped we hadn't forgotten anything.

Let us tell you, that shuttle is great! We wish all parks ran a shuttle like it. First of all, we loved the convenience of not having to worry about whether we would find parking. Second, the shuttle has a narrated tour on the way up the canyon but not on the way down. This is a really nice mix of getting to know the park and its landmarks and history and also having some quiet, peaceful time to stare out the windows and contemplate. Speaking of windows, these buses have enormous windows that wrap up the sides and onto the roof. Because you are traveling in a canyon, normal windows would only allow you to see the rock

The Virgin River is flanked by giants of stone in Zion National Park.

walls to your left and right. Not so with these special buses. You will see more from the bus than you ever would from your car.

We did have to make sure we were well supplied for the day before we headed out, but with a bit of planning, that is really no big deal. Another nice bonus is that there are plenty of water-bottle filling stations at some of the stops, so you won't run out of water! They are listed on the park map you receive when you come into the park.

The second thing you need to keep in mind when planning your visit is that the east entrance is only accessible through tunnels, one average-sized and one really long. Work began on the remarkable Zion–Mount Carmel Tunnel in 1927 and was completed in time for the opening ceremony in 1930. Driving through it is definitely exciting and awe inspiring, but large vehicles, including RVs, are restricted. You'll find more details in the Getting to Zion section but need to be aware of the restrictions if you plan to travel in an RV. For those not in oversized vehicles, this still means a delay in entering or leaving the park. There are rangers on either end who stop traffic in one direction in order to let large vehicles and other traffic pass in the other direction. Make sure to allow a bit of a time buffer for this possibility.

Another thing that makes Zion National Park unique is the visitor center. Located at the shuttle bus main terminal and the entrance to the campgrounds, it is beautiful, modern, and informative. We didn't leave nearly enough time to explore the somewhat maze-like compound. The areas outside the main building have wonderful displays addressing the nature and history of the park. They also explain some of the unique techniques the building's designers used to make the visitor center environmentally friendly. Our whole family was fascinated by them.

Inside you will find the usual gift shop, the ranger station with information about special events (ranger talks, guided hikes, night programs, Junior Ranger program), and the backcountry ranger station (for picking up backcountry permits, checking the weather conditions if you will be outside the main park area, etc.). What you won't find is the park's informational movie. While most parks have a video viewing area in the main visitor center, Zion National Park shows it up the road a bit at the park museum. We recommend that you save the park movie for the end of your trip. Although most adults like to gather as much information as possible before actually heading out to explore, kids are the opposite. We find that our kids think the park videos are boring unless they have already investigated the park and can recognize places in the video that they have personal experience discovering. You will find your children

Just one of the amazing views in Zion National Park

much better audience members if you wait until you're done exploring!

While at the visitor center, be sure to check out the schedule of ranger-led programs. There was only one program remaining in the season when we visited one fall, but it was the best program we went to that year! Not only was the information useful and fun for the kids ("Poisonous Stuff in the Desert") but it was held at the lodge at night. This was special for a few reasons. First, we got a pass allowing us to drive our vehicle past the "shuttle only" sign because the shuttle wasn't operating at night. The kids felt like rebels and renegades as we drove past that sign, even though we had a permit to do so. The second reason was that we got to spend time at the lodge. It's a beautiful old building and it was so romantic-looking all lit up at night. The biggest and best surprise came as we left the lodge after the program. We were there during a full moon, and the moonlight illuminated the white cliff faces across the river.

We were all in awe as we stood on the front lawn. It was surreal and moving. I have never seen anything like it. Obviously, we recommend trying to see a night program at the lodge if one is being offered.

There's another part of the park to the northwest, called Kolob Canyons. We investigated this area a little, but it's mostly wild and sometimes windy and not a very good place for kids. It's a good launching spot for some of the backcountry trips, and there are a few hikes as well as some amazing vistas. It's a short drive to check out most of the best views of a striking mountain range, but there weren't many activities to capture our kids' imaginations. We cover the Timber Creek Overlook Trail in that region (under Outside Zion Canyon), but for the most part, we focus on the Zion Canyon area.

Enough about all that. Let's get on to the good stuff: the trip planning! We've hiked all over Zion Canyon to bring you the best trips for your family. There is something for everyone here. Because of the canyon nature of the park, you should expect elevation gain in almost every trip. Some require less than others, but there is no way around having to climb a bit. Keep that in mind as you plan your Zion National Park vacation.

GETTING TO ZION

The options for traveling to Zion may seem obvious at first: car, RV, airplane, or a combination. However, you should take some things into consideration before making your choice. Keep in mind that you may want to explore the many fabulous national and state parks in the area. The number of these you choose to include in your itinerary may change how you want to travel. You may also think renting an RV is not for you, but there are many new types of RVs, and you may want to check into them before ruling them out.

However, for a visit to this park in particular, you need to know a few things about the tunnel on the east side if you will be using an RV. If your vehicle is 11'4" or taller, or 7'10" or wider (including anything sticking out like mirrors or awnings), you will need a tunnel permit. The permit can be purchased at the entrance station to the park ($15) and is good for two trips through the tunnel within seven days. Rangers stationed at the tunnel convert it from two-way to one-way traffic throughout the day when large vehicles need to pass through. In addition to the fee, oversized vehicles may go through only at certain times. The times below are typical, but exact dates vary from year to year. Check the park's website for the specific date you plan to visit.

> March–April: 8:00 AM to 7:00 PM
> May–August: 8:00 AM to 8:00 PM
> September: 8:00 AM to 7:00 PM
> October: 8:00 AM to 6:00 PM
> November–February: 8:00 AM to 4:30 PM, by advance reservation only

By car

From the west (Las Vegas, St. George), take I-15 north to exit 16, which is a right onto State Route 9 (in LaVerkin, Utah). Stay on SR 9 into Zion National Park.

From the northwest (Salt Lake City, Cedar City), take I-15 south to exit 27, then go left onto SR 17. Turn left (east) on SR 9 in LaVerkin and continue on SR 9 into the park.

From the south (Page, Arizona, or Kanab, Utah), take US Highway 89 north to Carmel Junction, Utah, and turn onto SR 9. Stay on SR 9 into Zion.

From the east (Bryce Canyon National Park), take SR 63 north. Go left on SR 12, then left again on US 89 south. From there, you will take a right onto SR 9 at Mount Carmel Junction and continue into the park.

By air

The international airports most convenient to Zion are Las Vegas (170 miles away) and Salt Lake City (311 miles away).

Regional airports include Saint George, Utah (49 miles away), and Cedar City, Utah (60 miles away).

ZION HIKING TRIPS

For organizational reasons, we list trips from south to north since the park entrances, the visitor center, and the park museum are on Zion's south side. You can do trips in any order, though, and you should think more about how much your family is capable of doing in one day than about completing trips in geographic order. Also, many hikes the National Park Service lists as separate hikes can easily be linked together. Here, we write them up as one hike if we feel they are best done as one.

There are a fairly limited number of hikes in Zion Canyon due to its steepness. There are also a few flat walks by the visitor center that we do not include here, as they are easy enough for anyone and need no special description.

Inside Zion Canyon (Shuttle Route)

We found plenty of adventure in Zion! Both in Zion Canyon, along the Virgin River, and outside that highly populated area, were hikes to capture our imagination and awe. The hikes in the main canyon, accessible by shuttle only, are frequented by the majority of visitors for a reason: they are stunning and exciting! The hikes in the other areas of the park met our need for adventurous routefinding and solitude.

Emerald Pools

This is a beautiful little hike that takes you to small hidden gems, including the Lower and Upper Emerald pools, along two different trails. The trail to the lower pool is easy enough for anyone to do, but starting immediately after that, the climb to the upper pool is fairly challenging. You can head back the way you came, but we recommend continuing on the Kayenta Trail to the next bus stop.

Even though it's paved, the path can be slippery when wet.

Distance: About a 2.5-mile loop (2 miles if you end at The Grotto instead of continuing along the road to the lodge where you started
Time: 2–3 hours, depending on time spent at the pools
Starting point: Zion Lodge shuttle stop

Our family loved this hike. It's a great family trip if you're able to hike for three hours and handle some moderate elevation gain. It can be broken into three sections, and at the end of either of the first two you can just return the way you came if you find you're unable to proceed onward. The first section is the hike

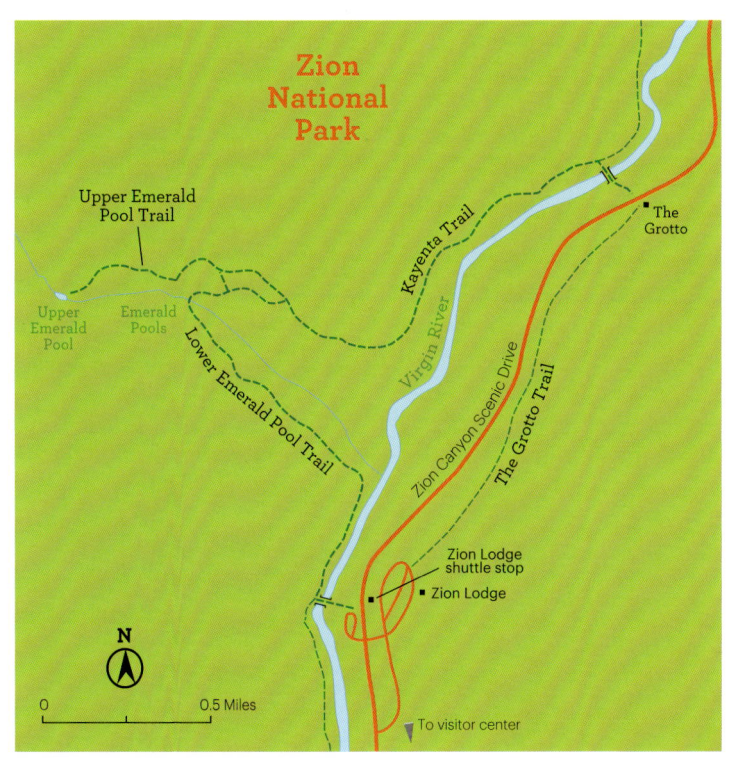

Emerald Pools hiking trails

ZION NATIONAL PARK   145

from the Zion Lodge shuttle drop-off to the Lower Emerald Pool. The second section proceeds on from the lower pool to the upper pool, and the last section returns you to the lodge via a different trail, the Kayenta Trail.

The first section is considered "easy" by the park service. It's a 1.2-mile paved and nicely shaded trail with minimal elevation gain. It leads to a series of small pools created by waterfalls of fine mist and water. The path heads under the curtain of mist, but be careful: it can be slippery at times. Overall, it's a nice stroll to a pretty water feature.

The second section leaves from the far side of the falls and heads up to the upper pool. This part of the trail was much more fun for our boys because it was rocky and they could hop along from boulder to boulder. It gains significant elevation and is more exposed to the sun, so bring adequate water and snacks. At one point you come to a junction with the Kayenta Trail. Keep left and continue heading up for now. On your way back down, you can take this fork and see some new territory. After hiking for only 0.5 mile past the first pools, you come to the Upper Emerald Pool.

This pool is a real surprise as you come around a corner and duck under the branches of a large tree. All of a sudden, you are in a box canyon with vertical walls rising all around you, and at the base is a clear, still pool. There is a sandy beach area at the entrance to the pool and some fun rocks for scrambling around on. There is a mix of shade and sun at midday, but due to the steepness and closeness of the canyon walls, the sun doesn't linger here. We brought a snack lunch and spent about an hour relaxing, climbing, eating, and playing in the water.

When you're ready to depart, head back out the same way you came. You will hike almost to the lower pool, but be watching for a small sign marked Kayenta Trail and a branching trail to your left. We had originally marked this trail on our map as a "no go," meaning we didn't think it sounded interesting enough to bother with. On our way back from the Emerald Pools we saw the cutoff and thought, "What can we lose?" Turns out it's a really great trail! It's a 1-mile trail that traverses the canyon up above the Virgin River. There are some drop-offs, but the trail is wide and flat, and we see very little danger of anyone actually falling off. We loved the views along the way. Being up high gives you a nice vantage point for this section of the canyon.

Our boys like to run ahead, and we liked that we could see them off and on as the trail curved around an outcropping. The only real elevation change is at the end, as the path drops down to the river and the road. Doing the hike in this direction means you have a more leisurely climb up and save the steeper section for going down.

At the bottom of the steep section, cross the bridge and you'll find yourself at The Grotto shuttle stop. If you want to walk back to the lodge, you can continue on The Grotto Trail along the river (another 0.5 mile) or, if your feet are tired, you can return by way of the shuttle bus. You can also catch the shuttle back to the campground or on to whichever hike is next for you.

View from behind the waterfall at Weeping Rock

Weeping Rock Trail

While short, this trail does involve some climbing, but the payoff is a cool spot where a veil of water droplets emerges from the rock and falls over you, creating a beautiful effect.

Distance: About 0.5 mile roundtrip
Time: About 30 minutes, depending on your stay at the top
Starting point: Weeping Rock shuttle stop

This is a short but fairly steep hike along a paved trail to a cliff face that is "weeping" water. You begin on the east side of the road where the northbound shuttle drops you off (if you arrive on the southbound bus, simply cross over to the east side). Cross through the parking area and look for the obvious trailhead. Many hikes begin from this same location, so look for the paved trail heading left, or up-canyon. Immediately start to climb the hill. Be sure to take advantage of the trailside plaques giving information about the plant life in the area (also a good excuse to stop and catch your breath!).

After about fifteen minutes, you reach the terminus of the trail at a steep rock face. Thin streams of water run off the top, forming a curtain of water droplets in front of an alcove in the base of the rock. There are handrails to hold as you cross little streams of water and duck under the overhang. This part is fun for kids and adults alike. You get to stand behind the water and look out over Zion Canyon. Stay as long as you like, then head back the way you came.

Hidden Canyon Trail

This trail has a lot of *wow* factor! You will earn it with a sustained and steep climb over switchbacks to reach the Hidden Canyon's start, but it's also the most memorable of all the trails we've hiked in this park. If you're scared of heights, however, it may not be for you.

As if the hike weren't amazing enough already—a hidden arch!

Distance: About 2.5 miles roundtrip
Time: About 2.5 hours, depending on how far you explore into the slot canyon at the top
Starting point: Weeping Rock shuttle stop

Although fairly strenuous, this trip was one of our kids' favorites (and ours!). Our youngest went in a baby backpack on Harley's back, and our next youngest was nine years old. None of our kids had any trouble with this, although you will want to be sure you trust your child to obey you promptly. You need to feel confident in your children's abilities and obedience when you encounter some serious drop-offs. If, after careful consideration, you feel the trail is within everyone's abilities, then don't hesitate further; we highly recommend this hike!

Leave from the Weeping Rock parking lot. The Weeping Rock trail is to your left; your route goes right. Start heading back toward the rock face at the east side of Zion Canyon. If you're out on a busy day, you can look up at the rock face and see people crisscrossing it like an army of tiny ants. That's where you're headed. This first part is the most tedious and physically challenging. Although paved or hard packed for good footing, it's steep. All 850 feet of elevation gain happens in this first part of the hike. Once you're pretty high up the cliff face, you will see a junction. The left fork heads off to Observation Point, another 6 miles distant. You want to take the right fork. Shortly after taking this branch, you get to the really fun part of the hike.

You're now traversing the canyon wall, heading in a down-canyon direction. There are stone stairs cut into the rocks and steep drop-offs on your down-cliff side. Make sure at this point that you have your children close and under control. As you move along the canyon wall you may begin to feel vertigo! A chain drilled into the rock gives you something to hold on to as the trail begins to look like something only a mountain goat would use. This, of course, was our boys' favorite part. Let's face it: kids like to challenge themselves, to dare themselves to do scary things. And it's our job to let them do that as safely as possible.

After about ten minutes of this type of hiking, the trail cuts back into a hidden slot canyon. It sort of peters out and you just have to make your way back into the canyon as far as you feel comfortable. Abby and the baby stayed at the entrance near a small pool of water. He loved throwing rocks and playing in the sand. The older boys and Harley went deeper into the canyon, all the way to a hidden rock arch! There was a lot of bouldering, scrambling, and problem solving involved.

Once you've enjoyed the rewards of your efforts and rested up, head back out the way you came in. We found that the trip in this direction looked totally new since we were facing up-canyon instead of down. This direction also took a lot less time because it's flat along the rock face and then goes down, down, down once you join the main trail again. You will end up at the same shuttle stop you left from.

Riverside Walk provides up-close views of the Virgin River and the surrounding canyon walls.

Riverside Walk–Temple of Sinawava

Because the trail is mostly paved and gains minimal elevation, it is suitable for anyone. You walk along the banks of the Virgin River in a lush riparian area with nice shade in spots, and the farther upstream you get, the more the canyon closes in on you.

Distance: About 2.2 miles roundtrip
Time: About 1.5 hours, depending on your stay at the top
Starting point: Temple of Sinawava shuttle stop

Such humble beginnings for the trail that heads to the top of Zion Canyon! It first leads to a section of the canyon called The Narrows, one of the most famous desert canyon experiences. (We go into more detail about this in the Other Trip Options section below.) The Riverside Walk is a paved path along the Virgin River. It has good footing and very little elevation gain (it's also wheelchair accessible) and is just beautiful. One note: even when we went in late fall, this trail was like a parade, there were so many people! If you're looking for desert solitude, skip this hike. But if you would like a nice afternoon stroll, hanging gardens, and possible wildlife sightings, then continue on.

As you leave the shuttle stop with the hordes on what appears to be a pilgrimage, follow the path to the left of the bathrooms. This trail, a wide paved path with good signage, is not hard to find. It's mostly shaded and follows the bank of the Virgin River. You will be able to see the river for most of your walk, and we saw various types of wildlife (squirrels, herons, deer) between us and the river, so keep your eyes open! There are also benches to rest on and interpretive signs along the way. One thing that caught our attention was the hanging gardens on the cliff side of the trail. At many places along the way there are ferns, moss, columbines, and other plants holding on to tiny niches in the rock surface. They gracefully hang down, softening the hard surface of the cliff.

Time for a bit of relaxing and experiencing

In a few places there are side trails that take you down to the river. We waited until we reached the end of the paved trail to spend time in the water, but any time kids are feeling bored or restless, take them to the water! There's nothing like throwing rocks and sailing stick boats to bring a kid's energy back up. Pair that with a snack and you will be good to go!

The "end" of the trail is only an end for those not heading into The Narrows. For those not going on, there are stone benches and plenty of shoreline for relaxing. After you finish enjoying your time in this beautiful area, return by the same trail you came up on.

Other Trip Options in Zion Canyon

Any research into trip options in Zion will eventually lead to information regarding The Narrows. As exciting as reports make it sound, this trip is not for children or inexperienced adults.

The Narrows

Distance: Various options: 9.5 miles out and back, 16-mile through-hike, two-day option
Time: Varies depending on trip; 8 hours or more
Starting point: Temple of Sinawava shuttle stop

The Narrows is a world-famous river canyoning experience. The Virgin River has carved out a spectacular canyon 16 miles long and up to 2000 feet deep. You trek past hanging gardens, sandstone grottoes, natural springs, and river-carved walls. This trip is the highlight of many people's vacations. However, it is also very remote and dangerous and requires that you wade through the river for most of the journey. The water is cold and the rocks are slippery. Flash flooding is a constant concern. Specialized equipment is needed. For most people this is not a do-it-yourself trip. If you feel it is a must-do, consider hiring a guide. Permits are required for any hiking above Orderville Canyon. Some permits can be reserved ahead of time, but others are given out in a daily drawing. If you hire guides, they will have their own permits. A note about children: the National Park Service's official publications state that children should not attempt The Narrows. While we are normally up for adventure, we know that long amounts of time in cold water and young kids don't go well together, so we have not done this hike. However, we have seen children, some appearing as young as seven years old, geared up with their parents and a guide. If you want to go and take your younger kids, please find a guide you trust and get their opinion.

Outside Zion Canyon

These trails are off the beaten path, offering more solitude than those inside Zion Canyon. However, because they are not well marked (or marked at all!), they require some level of comfort with routefinding.

Gifford Canyon (east side of Zion–Mount Carmel Tunnel)

Want to get away from the crowds and explore hidden areas of the park? Kids love an exploration and Gifford Canyon delivers! Since the hikes are in river bottoms, elevation gains are minimal.

Distance: 1–3 miles
Time: 1–2 hours
Starting point: Canyon Overlook Trail parking area, on the east side of the long Zion–Mount Carmel Tunnel. There are two parking areas, one for cars going in each direction. Either is fine to use; the trail leaves from the one on the south side of the road, immediately outside the tunnel. This is also where the bathrooms are.

Gifford Canyon is a special and secluded "hanging" canyon, so labeled because it's about 25 feet above the river that it eventually drains into. The canyon itself is basically flat, but accessing it is work for fairly strong scramblers, as you need to scale a short but steep rocky bank. This is not a canyon for small children who are walking on their own (we carried our two-year-old in the baby backpack) or older people unsteady on their feet. However, if you're willing to brave the entry climb, you will be well rewarded.

To access Gifford Canyon, go to the parking lot immediately east of the tunnel and on the south side of the road to locate a "goat trail" heading down behind the bathrooms. It took us a bit of looking around and asking the tunnel ranger about it, but we did find it. Before you head down, you have a great opportunity to orient yourself to where you'll be headed. If you look out behind the bathrooms, you will see the river bottom below, stretching to the left and right of you. Immediately in front of you and on the opposite side of the river is a large, rocky hump. That will be your challenge: you need to get down to the river bottom, then scale the hump, ending up on the right-hand side as you're looking at it. That's where you will find Gifford. Now you're ready to start in!

Head down the small, rocky trail to the river bottom below. It's a bit of a sliding scramble, so be quick on your toes. Once at the bottom, head across to the large hump, now looming above you. There is no trail, so you must pick your way. You are headed to the right side, but we found it easier to start up the left and then cross over toward the top. Our kids were fine, but I was worried the whole time we were climbing!

As you come over the top of the hump, you find a beautiful and remote sandy creek bottom (dry when we were there in the fall). It's a wide bottom, with scattered sun and shade, that you can wander up as far or long as you want to. We saw countless animal tracks in the sand, and it was such fun to try to identify what had been there and what they might have been doing.

The boys ran and climbed and tried to do *Matrix*-style moves on the sandstone boulders we found. We saw no sign of other people having been there. In a park as crowded as Zion, this is a rarity. We spent a very relaxing afternoon in Gifford and recommend it to anyone able to make the initial scramble. When you're done, head back out the way you came. Be careful on the way down the hump!

Side note: It's fun to explore up or down the main river bottom you encounter below the bathrooms. This part of the river holds water year-round in spots, so you may not be able to get very far. But we found a lot of fun mud, dried mud curls, boulders, and caves to explore when we were there. Remember that it's easier to get up than it is to get down! We had some kids trying to go places we weren't sure they could get down from, so keep an eye on yours.

Hidden Garden Canyon (east side of Zion–Mount Carmel Tunnel)

Feel as though you're discovering a hidden treasure for the first time with this cool adventure. The terrain is easy, although you do have to routefind a bit. But it will all be in glorious shade! Caution: Flash flooding in desert canyons is always a real danger. Please make sure you've checked the weather report and spoken with a ranger before going off into any desert canyon. Even rain 40 miles away can cause flooding in your area. Also, when heading off-trail, it's a good idea to leave a note in your vehicle about where you're headed. Then if anything goes wrong, it's easier to find you. We recommend this trip because we feel it's very safe and fun, but you should always take precautions when exploring nature!

Distance: 1–2 miles, depending on how far up the canyon you go
Time: 1–3 hours. Afternoon is a good time to go, as this is a shady hike in a cool canyon.
Starting point: Parking area on the west side of the shorter, east tunnel. There are parking areas on either side of the road, and either one works. (See the Getting to Zion section for more information on the tunnels in Zion.)

This is a little-known, on-your-own, off-the-beaten-path hike. In fact, when we tried to ask people about this "hidden garden" canyon hike we'd heard about, no one knew what we were talking about. We also didn't find reference to it in the guidebooks we were using. What's more exciting to a kid than the feeling of being the first explorer in a new area? Our kids loved everything about this hike, and so did we!

Begin in either of two parking areas on the west side (the park side) of the smaller tunnel. You're going to head down from the parking area, and you can do that on either side. If you head down the north (right side, as you face the park), you will get to take your kids through a very cool tunnel as you pass under the

You'll find the entrance for Hidden Canyon behind the largest pine tree.

road. We took the south side down and then on the way back passed through the tunnel and came up the north side. Both sides were fine. You will need to scramble and be willing to slide a bit. There is no trail, so make sure everyone is comfortable with this. This is the hardest part of the hike.

Once you arrive at the bottom, head south (downstream) in the sandy drainage until you encounter the main river bottom. It will be quite clear when you get there from this direction, but you need to take a moment to mark this spot for yourself, as it is easy to miss when you're coming back. (Don't panic if you miss it. You will just have headed too far in the main channel and need to come back upstream until you see the turn.) When you find the main riverbed, turn left, or upstream. In the fall, this river bottom was dry, though we did find pockets of water.

Look for a side canyon that has beautiful natural gardens. The indicator that you've found it is a huge pine tree on the right (as you are heading upstream). As you walk along, you will see many trees and be asking yourself, "Is this the one?" or "Maybe this is it?" You will know when you see the one you seek. It's the biggest pine tree we've ever seen. It's guarding the entrance to the beautiful and secluded canyon you're looking for. When you find it, sneak behind it and you will see the start of the hidden gardens.

This little side canyon isn't classified as a slot canyon; if a slot canyon is what your kids want, look up and to the left of the side canyon just as you enter it. Our boys found an undiscovered (or at least unnamed) slot they had to explore. We headed up and into the mouth, and boy, was it tight! It's definitely a side-shimmy if there ever was one! The tiny slot heads back for about 25 yards, then takes a sharp turn. You can follow it all the way to the back, where it ends on a high ledge. Our boys named this "Knife-Cut Canyon Slot."

Return to the Hidden Garden side canyon and proceed up and away from the main riverbed. This is a great place to let your kids run wild. They won't disturb anyone, and they can't get lost. They are in a canyon, after all. There are many downed trees that make for great climbing and scrambling, and there are beautiful flowers and plants. The fall colors were spectacular when we were there. Enjoy your time and then head back the way you came.

Timber Creek Overlook Trail (Kolob Canyons)

If you take the time to visit the northwest portion of the park, then you might as well include this short hike to a nice overlook of the impressive mountains across the way.

Distance: 1 mile
Time: 30 minutes–1 hour
Starting point: Kolob Canyons Road

The trail leaves the back side of the Kolob Canyons Viewpoint parking lot and climbs at an easy pace up to the top of a hill where you get impressive views of the mountains on the other side of the canyon. Although this trail is more primitive than those in the higher-traffic areas of the park, you will have no problem following it as you head uphill. It's a nice chance to stretch your legs a bit. Head back down once you've taken enough pictures.

OTHER ACTIVITIES IN ZION

There are a few other options, in addition to hiking, for enjoying Zion National Park.

Wildlife viewing

Although the park's geography makes it a bit difficult to spot wildlife, you can find opportunities if you look hard enough. This sort of rocky canyon is often home to bighorn sheep, and Zion Canyon is no exception. We had the best luck sighting them on the east side of the park, even before we went through the big tunnel. From the parking lot for the Canyon Overlook Trail, just east of the big tunnel, look to the cliff face that surrounds the

The mountains of Kolob Canyon

parking lot and you're very likely to see part of the herd that calls this spot home.

Birds are also drawn to this type of canyon, and 288 bird species are found here. You can pick up birding guides with bird checklists at the visitor center. You may be lucky enough to see peregrine falcons, California condors, or bald eagles soaring from the heights of the cliffs.

Rock climbing

Zion National Park is well-known for its world-class rock climbing. The canyon's sandstone walls make for incredible opportunities. However, the climbs in the park are mostly for very experienced climbers. There are few top-rope routes and no sport climbs. No permits are required for day climbs, but you do need to check which areas may be closed for nesting peregrine falcons. If you just like to live vicariously, you may be able to catch glimpses of others climbing, especially on your way to the Temple of Sinawava.

Bicycling

Biking is only permitted on roadways (though not at all in the Zion–Mount Carmel Tunnel) and the Pa'rus Trail. Shuttle buses have racks for at least two bicycles at a time, and you may bike on the canyon roads, though they are narrow and therefore may not be safe for small children. We found the bus drivers were very alert to cyclists, and since there are really no other vehicles on the upper roads, you may deem it safe for your kids to ride.

Horseback riding

Guided horseback rides leave from the corral near the Emerald Pools trailhead. There are special restrictions for using private stock, so be sure to check that out carefully if you plan to bring your own horse.

Canyoneering

Zion is home to many really great canyons that are a lot of fun to explore. The Narrows and The Subway are two of the best known. Please keep in mind that many of these require special gear and advanced technical skills. They also require permits.

Backpacking

There are fun areas to explore in the Zion backcountry, but you will need to obtain a permit to do so. This is not a park we recommend for families to begin their backpacking journey. Due to the desert nature of the park, you will have to carry a lot of your own water. Also, many dangers, from flash flooding to drastic temperature swings, make Zion tricky for the inexperienced. See the park website for details on permits and regulations. We also really enjoyed and appreciated the book *Utah's Incredible Backcountry Trails*. You can find a bunch of the trip reports from the book online.

ZION CAMPING AND LODGING

Zion National Park has two options for overnight guests. The first is the Zion Lodge. The other is to camp in one of three campgrounds (two are in the main park area and one is on the Kolob Terrace Road on the north side of the park).

Zion Lodge

Three miles up Zion Scenic Drive, the lodge is a beautiful, historic log building nestled at the base of Zion Canyon's majestic walls. The only private vehicles allowed on this road are those with a special pass for people staying at the lodge (see our hint for how to get a permit without staying at the lodge in the park overview at the beginning of this chapter). Advance reservations are recommended and can be made through Xanterra Parks & Resorts. They have rooms, cabins, and suites to choose from. If you stay at the lodge, you will find nature at your doorstep!

Campgrounds

There are two campground options in the main part of the park: Watchman and South. Both campgrounds fill up by early afternoon most days of the year, so you will want to have reservations or get there early. They offer little shade, so be prepared with some means of creating your own shade.

Watchman Campground

This campground is 0.25 mile from the park's south entrance, adjacent to the visitor center. The sites here (176 regular sites, 2 wheelchair-accessible sites, and 6 group sites) can accommodate tents or RVs requiring electrical hook-ups (no generators allowed). Reservations for stays from March to November are available six months in advance. The last time we visited the park, we were unable to get reservations for a regular car-camping site, but there were still many walk-in sites available. We had never done a walk-in site before and weren't sure how that would work, what with all the gear we generally haul around. We took the reservation and it worked out fine. You park and have to walk a very short distance on a paved path to your site. We really enjoyed our site, and our car was a stone's throw away. It's an option to consider if regular car-camping sites are filled up. The facilities are very clean and modern. There are no showers, but they do have a very nice sink for dish washing.

South Campground

This campground is next to Watchman, 0.5 mile from the south entrance. It boasts 127 campsites (3 are wheelchair accessible), which are available on a first come, first served basis. You will not find hook-ups here for your RV, but you can use a generator if you have one. This is a good option if you were unable to get reservations ahead of time, but you need to get there as early in the day as possible to increase your chances of securing a site.

Lava Point Campground

This little-known campground is in the park's Kolob Terrace region, on the Kolob Terrace Road. It's about an hour away from the main Zion Canyon area. Its six primitive sites are available on a first come, first served basis. Only pit toilets and trash cans are provided. No water is available. Keep in mind that this part of the park is at a much higher elevation than the Zion Canyon area (the campground is at 7890 feet). This means temperatures will be much colder than at the other two campgrounds. These six sites would be a rustic last option if you were unable to secure a site in one of the other two campgrounds.

DAY TRIP: GRAND CANYON NATIONAL PARK–NORTH RIM

At some point on our last trip, one of us looked at a map and realized how close to the Grand Canyon we would be while at Zion National Park. When we ran into a problem getting a permit for a hike we had planned on doing, we immediately said, "Let's go to the Grand Canyon instead!"

A mere two hours to the south of Zion National Park, the North Rim of the Grand Canyon is a very doable day trip. Now, the Grand Canyon deserves more than a day. As with all national parks, you could devote an entire lifetime to exploring it. But if your main visit is planned around Zion National Park, what a bonus to be able to "stop by" such a tremendous national site!

Below, we share some easy and quick hikes that your family could do in a one-day visit. Don't forget that ranger programs and the Junior Ranger program are also going on. Make sure to start your visit with a stop at the visitor center to find out what ranger talks or walks are happening that day and to pick up a Junior Ranger book. Even with only one day, our kids were able to complete the program requirements. One final reminder: Arizona does not change clocks during daylight saving time. All of the Grand Canyon's program times and visitor center hours may be different than the time you're on in Utah. Be sure to synchronize your watch with local time when you arrive.

The North Rim of the Grand Canyon offers a dramatically different experience than what people generally expect. When most people think about visiting the Grand Canyon, they have the South Rim in mind, often without even realizing it. Many of the pictures we see and videos we watch represent the South Rim much more than the North Rim. The North Rim surprises you with its aspen forests, cool temperatures, high elevation, and relative solitude. As you drive into the park, you find yourself passing through green meadows and conifer forests mingling with aspen groves. You're likely to see deer, but keep a look out for buffalo, bear, turkeys, and coyotes as well.

There are fewer annual visitors on this side of the canyon, so it's not as commercialized or busy. Be sure to check in at the visitor center, which is off the main road in the complex of buildings that make up the Grand Canyon Lodge. The lodge itself is one of the most spectacular we've seen.

Looking back at the lodge from Bright Angel Trail

Many of the ranger talks are held on the lodge's back porch, but even if you aren't going to one of those, be sure to check out the porch anyway. You can order something cool to drink while you sit in a comfortable chair, or you're welcome to bring your own drinks or snacks. The views are outstanding.

Finally, while we always encourage families to get out of their cars and let their kids experience parks, sometimes just a drive is worth it. We loved the scenic drives out to Point Imperial (the North Rim's highest point) and Cape Royal. You have big canyon views along the way, and where there aren't views, you see beautiful aspen groves and, quite possibly, wildlife. If you hike on the Cape Royal Trail (below), you will get to do this drive anyway. You should have time to do this drive and the hikes below and still hear a ranger talk—all in a single day!

North Rim of Grand Canyon National Park Hiking Trips

Below we offer a handful of easy and short hikes to give you a taste of what this side of the Grand Canyon has to offer.

Cape Royal Trail

Short and easy with spectacular views, this is a hike anyone could (and should) do.

Distance: 0.6 mile roundtrip
Time: 1 hour
Starting point: Cape Royal parking area, southeast side

This hike is pretty short but takes you out from among the juniper forests to the rim of the canyon. It's paved and relatively flat. We found the interpretive signs along the way quite worth reading, especially out at the end. As you hike out of the scrub forest, you are rewarded with dramatic views of the canyon, Angels Window (a natural stone window below the canyon rim), and the Colorado River far below in the bottom of the canyon. A short spur takes you out onto the top of Angels Window. After admiring the view, return the way you came.

Cliff Springs Trail

Another short hike—this time to a cool hanging cliff you can walk under. It shows you another side of Grand Canyon, away from the huge and distant vistas—here it's more up close and personal.

Distance: 1 mile roundtrip
Time: 1.5 to 2 hours
Starting point: Across from a small pullout area 0.3 mile north of the Cape Royal trailhead (pullout is on the west side of the road on a curve)

A hidden gem of a hike, the Cliff Springs Trail starts out in a coniferous forest and heads gently downhill past an ancient granary site and eventually to an overhanging sandstone alcove. The alcove is full of water seeps and springs (don't drink the water!) and hanging gardens. You may spot animal tracks near the wet areas. If you continue along under the alcove, you will come to a spot with a unique perspective of the canyon itself. This would make a great picnic spot, so bring along some food and drink, and enjoy a cool and private place. The trail looks seldom used and feels very secluded. We loved it and think your kids (and you) will too!

Walhalla Overlook

This is a very short stroll to view old stone foundations from Native American dwellings.

Distance: None, just an overlook along a parking area
Time: 10 minutes
Starting point: Walhalla Overlook parking area, near Cape Royal

Historic sites along the way make this short stop at Walhalla Overlook worthwhile.

Although not a traditional hike, Walhalla Overlook is worth a visit. This overlook provides you with not only a view of the canyon from the rim but also a historical perspective on the ancient peoples who once lived on the Walhalla Plateau. The park service provides a flyer with interpretive information at the site.

Bright Angel Trail

Very big views await at the end of the very short trail. If you have any time to spend around the visitor center, take the time to make this short walk; you'll be glad you did.

Distance: 0.5 mile roundtrip
Time: 1 hour
Starting point: Visitor center parking area or the back porch of the lodge

---

This is a high-traffic, paved trail heading from the lodge and visitor center out to Bright Angel Point. There is some slight elevation gain and loss, but most people will be able to do it. Be prepared to keep close track of small children, as there are some narrow spots with steep drop-offs. Despite the number of people and the potential for falling, this is a fantastic trail with great views, perfect for a one-day visit.

Hike along the rim for a few minutes and then head out on a narrow peninsula of land jutting over the canyon. There are places to climb up rocks and get a new perspective, which kids love. Out at the point, try to spot the North Kaibab Trail as it snakes its way to the bottom of the canyon; Phantom Ranch, a stop-over spot at the bottom; and the Colorado River, looking like a silver ribbon winding its way through the canyon bottom.

Inside Double Arch (Arches National Park)

SAFETY IN THE PARKS

The desert is a beautiful place to visit, but it comes with its own challenges. Familiarizing yourself with the main concerns of desert exploring will help you prepare yourself and your family for a safe and relaxing vacation in the desert.

TEMPERATURE

You will be in extreme elements, either hot or cold, and it's easy to experience severe symptoms of overexposure to the cold or sun and not realize it at first. The desert environment is unlike any other, with temperatures that can fluctuate 50 degrees or more in one day! It's not uncommon to be sweating at midday and shivering an hour after the sun goes down. A storm can blow in quickly and leave you cold and wet sooner than you would believe possible. And because kids have smaller body masses, their bodies have a harder time maintaining appropriate temperatures.

The weather may also impact your choice of sleeping accommodations. We almost always camp, but if the weather is extremely hot or cold, the refuge of a lodge or a hotel room can keep your kids in high spirits. There is nothing like a hot shower after a cold hike, or a dip in a cool swimming pool in the middle of a sweltering summer day. A little air conditioning may help you get a good night's sleep so that you're ready to tackle the trails in the morning cool of the following day.

Heat

To minimize the harmful effects of being in a hot desert environment, it's wise to bring and wear lightweight clothing that covers your arms and legs. Also, wear a hat and sunglasses.

On hot days, it's best to plan more strenuous activities for early and late in the day, when temperatures are cooler. If you still want to hike midday, seek out hikes that take you near steep canyon walls, which provide some relief from the sun. Bring lots of water and sunscreen, and wear loose-fitting clothes that dry from perspiration quickly and also offer protection from the sun's rays. A wide-brimmed hat is effective in shading your skin and eyes from the sun, and keeping you cool.

HEAT EXHAUSTION

If you're traveling with kids, you're likely visiting in the summer, and that means the daytime highs will most likely be quite warm. You may find yourself hiking farther than usual as you take in the amazing sights in these parks, and you may suddenly realize someone in your group has overdone it in the heat and isn't looking too good.

Learning to recognize heat exhaustion is fairly straightforward. Victims may feel lethargic, confused, or weak. As the condition progresses, there will be a headache and muscle cramps, and it can escalate to nausea and vomiting. The treatment is to move the victim out of the sun and to a cooler location, reduce the level of activity, and get hydrated with water or sports drinks.

If heat exhaustion is left unchecked, the body eventually loses its ability to regulate temperature. The victim will be in an altered mental state and may have a seizure, and his skin will cease to sweat and will feel cool and clammy with goose bumps even on a hot day. This is heatstroke, a life-threatening condition, and emergency medical treatment should be sought immediately.

Cold

Most of Utah's national parks are on the Colorado Plateau, which is a high desert in every sense of the word. The climate is dry and the terrain is quite high in elevation. As a result, evenings in the parks can get quite chilly, especially if you're there in the shoulder seasons.

You can compensate for the cold by dressing in layers, but you don't need to go overboard with technical gear. A basic, inexpensive fleece jacket is light to carry and offers excellent insulation. Wool socks have come a long way in recent years, and a merino wool hiking sock will not only regulate your temperature but also provide good protection against blisters due to its natural wicking abilities. Another thing to keep in mind is that you can lose a good deal of heat from your head. This means that even a small, lightweight hat thrown in your bag can be a real lifesaver if you find yourself getting chilled. When we set out on a hike in the desert, we bring layers of clothes. We also like to carry a fleece skullcap for each kid.

One day we set out on a hike that seemed very straightforward. At some point we lost track of the trail in the sagebrush and misjudged how far along we were. As the sun was sinking lower in the sky and the kids were starting to feel chilled and hungry, we decided it was faster to keep going than to backtrack. As we walked and walked, we began to get nervous, but stopping to pull out warmer layers helped everyone feel better and continue along the trail. We got back much later than we had planned but averted any major disaster by having appropriate additional clothing with us.

DEHYDRATION

Dehydration is a very real possibility in this environment, and that is true whether it's hot or cold. We associate it with warm temperatures, but cold air is actually very dry, and the simple act of breathing in cold temperatures can cause you to lose a lot of water (why do you think you can "see your breath" when it's cold?). Summer and winter in the deserts of Utah are dry, so you will be losing water from sweat and from breathing.

There are many opinions on the amount of water that a typical person needs each day, but most health authorities recommend at least two liters or quarts of water per day. This equates to sixty-four ounces. Soda drinks aren't the same! This guideline is for kids ages nine and up—smaller children can get by with a little bit less. Children four to eight years old can typically get by on five cups, or forty ounces, of water per day.

A typical Nalgene-style bottle is one liter, so a good practice is to fill one up for each person in the morning and commit to drinking them all by lunch. Then fill them up again and drink them all again by dinner. If you keep that up at a minimum, you should be in pretty good shape; but if you're going on long or strenuous hikes, you will need to boost your water intake accordingly.

FLASH FLOODS

Another very real danger of the desert is flash flooding. It's counterintuitive, but a great deal of the region's moisture actually comes in late summer due to the monsoon season. This results in localized but intense rainstorms that can dump a great deal of moisture in a short amount of time. The rock and clay of this region is often baked so hard that the rainfall cannot readily penetrate the surface and be absorbed, so the water rushes downhill and creates flash flooding.

One thing many people are unaware of is that a flash flood can occur where you are even if the rain is far away! Rain many miles away can begin to fill canyons and arroyos. As it travels along, it picks up logs, trees, rocks, and other flotsam. By the time it gets to you, it can be a very dangerous force that gives you no warning. Most visitor centers will publish information on the forecast that includes the likelihood of these events, so pay them heed.

You can do a lot to avoid this danger. Your best defense is to check in with rangers before heading out on any adventures.

Rock scrambling is all part of the fun.

They are well aware of the dangers of flash floods, how they form, and what areas will be safe for you to travel in. We always check in, especially when we may be exploring trails less traveled or going on all-day hikes.

The second thing you should do is leave an outline of your hiking plans (where, how long, how many people, etc.) in your car. That way if there is an emergency evacuation in a certain area and the rangers see your car still there, they can break in and know where to look for you.

If by some chance you do find yourself in a flood, you need to get to high ground immediately. Leave anything that might slow you down or that is not necessary in an emergency survival situation and go to higher ground. Walls of flash-flood waters have been known to reach 10 to 30 feet high. You need to get as high as you can (unless there is also lightning—then you need to get as high as you can without being the highest thing in the area).

SNAKEBITES

The desert is filled with remarkable creatures that have learned to live in extreme conditions. Snakes are such creatures. They work hard to survive and will therefore flee if given the chance. If you come upon a snake sunning itself, do what you can to back away very slowly and go around, giving it a wide berth.

If for some reason you're bitten, the number one thing you can do to improve your chances of surviving with minimal damage is to remain calm. If your heart begins to beat rapidly, the venom will also spread more rapidly. Keep hydrated, still, and calm while help is found. You will need to get to a hospital as soon as possible. That's it. You don't need to cut an X across the bite, suck it, use snakebite antivenin, or anything else. Your path to the least damage is much simpler.

FIRST-AID KITS

Having a first-aid kit in your car will bring peace of mind, and if you're planning on hiking or backpacking, definitely bring a simple first-aid kit with you. Many commercial options are available online or from any pharmacy or outdoors store, but there are some special considerations for families as well. Many "full-featured" kits contain so many bulky and heavy items that you would never want to carry them in your daypack. So when you look for kits online, add keywords like "hiking" or "backpacking" so that you find smaller kits with lighter items inside. Even "camping" first-aid kits are so large that they are best left back at camp. A first-aid kit is only worthwhile if you actually bring it along, and a big, bulky kit is too likely to be left behind.

If you are the do-it-yourself type, you can also create your own kit with a few basic items. See the checklist in the following section.

DISCLAIMER

Utah's national parks are not amusement parks; they are wild places. While that is one of their greatest attractions, it also carries with it certain risks. We have done our best to provide reasonable advice and guidance on how to have a fun, safe, adventurous family vacation in the parks, but there is no way we can write a book that is a substitute for the reader's sound judgment. Conditions in the desert can change quickly, and only you can respond to those changes; a book cannot. Every family is made up of members with differing strengths and weaknesses. You know your family, and we do not. So do your research and make your plans, and then make the right decisions when you're in the parks and faced with your specific circumstances. We are confident that with the right preparation and planning, you will have a safe and excellent vacation, but we cannot *guarantee* that outcome.

TRAVEL CHECKLISTS

WILDLIFE SPOTTING CHECKLISTS

Common animals in Arches National Park

- ☐ Desert cottontail rabbit
- ☐ Kangaroo rat
- ☐ Mule deer
- ☐ Bighorn sheep
- ☐ Turkey vulture
- ☐ Raven
- ☐ White-throated swift
- ☐ Pinyon jay
- ☐ Peregrine falcon
- ☐ Toad (various)
- ☐ Snake (various)
- ☐ Lizard (various)

Common animals in Canyonlands National Park

- ☐ Desert cottontail rabbit
- ☐ Kangaroo rat
- ☐ Mule deer
- ☐ Bighorn sheep
- ☐ Turkey vulture
- ☐ Raven
- ☐ White-throated swift
- ☐ Pinyon jay
- ☐ Peregrine falcon
- ☐ Toad (various)
- ☐ Snake (various)
- ☐ Lizard (various)

Common animals in Capitol Reef National Park

- ☐ Mule deer
- ☐ Ringtail

- ☐ Gray fox
- ☐ Canyon bat
- ☐ Squirrel
- ☐ Yellow-bellied marmot
- ☐ Desert bighorn sheep
- ☐ Toad (various)
- ☐ Snake (various)
- ☐ Lizard (various)
- ☐ Turkey vulture
- ☐ Raven
- ☐ Pinyon jay

Common animals in Bryce Canyon National Park

- ☐ Golden-mantled ground squirrel
- ☐ Utah prairie dog
- ☐ Pronghorn antelope
- ☐ Mule deer
- ☐ Ringtail
- ☐ Coyote
- ☐ Toad (various)
- ☐ Snake (various)
- ☐ Lizard (various)
- ☐ Turkey vulture
- ☐ Raven
- ☐ Pinyon jay

Common animals in Zion National Park

- ☐ Desert cottontail rabbit
- ☐ Rock squirrel
- ☐ Ringtail
- ☐ Mule deer
- ☐ Bighorn sheep
- ☐ Toad (various)
- ☐ Snake (various)
- ☐ Lizard (various)
- ☐ Peregrine falcon
- ☐ Turkey vulture
- ☐ Raven
- ☐ Pinyon jay

FIRST-AID KIT CHECKLIST

Here is what we would recommend for a very basic kit, all kept in a quart-size, sealable plastic bag:

- ☐ Tweezers. These are for splinters; you may have some already on your pocketknife.
- ☐ Safety pins. These can secure bandage wraps and be used to create arm slings, etc. Get larger ones that are robust—old baby-diaper pins are the best.
- ☐ Bandannas. These can be used for splints, slings, or to dip in water to cool off someone getting too hot.
- ☐ Adhesive bandages of various sizes and shapes
- ☐ Medical tape and gauze bandages for larger wounds
- ☐ Antibiotic ointment
- ☐ Antiseptic wipes
- ☐ Moleskin for blisters. Duct tape works just as well.
- ☐ Elastic bandage
- ☐ Medication. Ibuprofen and naproxen sodium, also called NSAIDs, help prevent swelling in addition to being pain relievers.
- ☐ Antihistamine for allergic reactions

DAY HIKING CHECKLIST
The 10 Essentials

1. Navigation: map, compass, GPS
2. Headlamp or flashlight, with spare batteries
3. Sun protection: sunscreen, lip balm, sunglasses
4. First-aid kit and moleskin or tape
5. Knife
6. Fire: matches or lighter, waterproof container
7. Shelter: rain jackets at a minimum, a tarp or bivy sack
8. Extra food and snacks, sugary and salty, especially for kids!
9. Extra water: full water bottles or hydration system (in the desert, water probably won't be available along the way, so a filter or purifying tablets likely aren't going to help)
10. Extra clothes: jacket, vest, pants, gloves, hat

Other useful items to consider

- Bear spray
- Repair kit: knife or multi-tool, duct tape, twine
- Day pack
- Toilet paper!
- Camera
- Binoculars
- Insect repellent

RESOURCES

Arches National Park
PO Box 907
Moab, UT 84532
(435) 719-2299
www.nps.gov/arch/index.htm

Interactive Arches map
www.nps.gov/arch/planyourvisit/maps.htm

Nearby Services
Many services are available in the town of Moab, Utah.

Moab Area Travel Council
PO Box 550
Moab, UT 84532
www.discovermoab.com

Moab Information Center
25 East Center Street
Moab, UT 84532
(435) 259-8825

Additionally, an internet search will point you toward many outfitters based in the Moab area. They offer all sorts of adventure expeditions as well as amenities including showers, camping, and laundry.

Canyonlands National Park
2282 Resource Blvd.
Moab, UT 84532
(435) 719-2313
www.nps.gov/cany/index.htm

Interactive Canyonlands map
www.nps.gov/cany/planyourvisit/maps.htm

Canyonlands backcountry permits for cycling and camping
www.nps.gov/planyourvisit/backcountrypermits.htm

Nearby Services
Many services are available in the town of Moab, Utah.

Moab Area Travel Council
PO Box 550
Moab, UT 84532
www.discovermoab.com

Moab Information Center
25 East Center St.
Moab, UT 84532
(435) 259-8825

Additionally, an internet search will point you toward many outfitters based in the Moab area. They offer all sorts of adventure expeditions as well as amenities including showers, camping, and laundry.

Capitol Reef National Park
HC 70, Box 15
Torrey, UT 84775
(435) 425-3791
www.nps.gov/care/index.htm

Interactive Capitol Reef map
www.nps.gov/care/planyourvisit/maps.htm

Nearby Services
The closest town is Torrey, Utah, about 5 miles west of the park. It has all services, including a number of hotels and restaurants.

Wayne County Travel Council Information Center
12 UT-24

Torrey, UT 84775
(435) 425-3365
www.capitolreef.org

Bryce Canyon National Park

PO Box 640201
Bryce, UT 84764
(435) 834-5322
www.nps.gov/brca/index.htm
Bryce Canyon campground reservations: www.recreation.gov

Nearby Services

The Ruby's Inn complex (www.rubysinn.com) just north of the park entrance offers lodging, restaurants, an RV park, and camping, as well as a general store with a gas station across the street. A number of hotels line State Route 12 near the park.

Zion National Park

1 Zion Park Blvd.
State Route 9
Springdale, UT 84767
(435) 772-3256
www.nps.gov/zion/index.htm

Additional Zion Hikes

Utah's Incredible Backcountry Trails
www.utahtrails.com

Nearby Services

Springdale, Utah, is just outside the park and has many hotels, restaurants, outfitters, and other amenities including showers and laundry.

Springdale and Zion Canyon Visitor Center
1101 Zion Park Blvd.
Springdale, UT 84767
www.zionnationalpark.com
Zion Canyon Visitors Bureau
www.zionpark.com

Other Resources

Authors' website
www.our4outdoors.com

Campsite Reservations
www.recreation.gov

Horse Trail Rides
www.canyonrides.com

Lodging
Bryce Canyon Lodge
www.brycecanyonforever.com
(877) 386-4383

Xanterra Parks and Resorts
www.zionlodge.com
(435) 772-7700

Rafting
Colorado River (Cataract Canyon)
www.utah.com/raft/rivers/cataract.htm

Colorado River (Westwater Canyon)
www.utah.com/raft/rivers/westwater.htm

Green River (Desolation and Gray Canyons)
www.utah.com/raft/rivers/desolation.htm

INDEX

Arches National Park 17–18, 26, 30, 35–31, 44–69
    campgrounds in 69
    getting to 49
    hikes in 49–66

backpacking 68, 106, 132–33, 162
bicycling 68, 82–83, 106, 162
Bright Angel Trail 169
Bristlecone Loop 126–28
Broken Arch–Tapestry Arch Loop 52–54
Bryce Canyon National Park 18, 24, 29, 38–40, 111–135
    campgrounds in 133–35
    getting to 115–17
    hikes in 117–31
    lodges in 133

campgrounds 69, 85, 109–10, 134–35, 164
canyoneering 106, 162
Canyonlands National Park 17–18, 26–27, 30–31, 37–38, 70–85
    campgrounds in 85
    getting to 72–74
    hikes in 74–81
Cape Royal Trail 167
Capitol Reef National Park 17–18, 24, 29, 31, 38, 86–110
    campgrounds in 107–10
    getting to 89–90
    hikes in 90–106
Cassidy Arch 96–100

Cathedral Valley Campground 110
Cedar Breaks National Monument 34
Cedar Mesa Campground 109
Cliff Springs Trail 167–68
Cohab Canyon 92–95

Dark Rangers 40
Delicate Arch 59–62
Devils Garden Campground 69
Devils Garden Trail 56, 57–59
Double Arch 65–66
Double O Arch 57–59

Emerald Pool 143–47

Fairyland Loop 130–31
flash floods 18, 154, 156, 162, 174–77
four-wheel-driving 33, 34, 83
Fruita Campground 109

Gifford Canyon 155–56
Gifford House 88–89, 109
Grand Canyon (north rim) 24, 29, 34, 164–69
Grand Staircase–Escalante National Monument 32
Grand View Point 76–78
Grand Wash 95–96
Green River Overlook 81

Headquarters Canyon 100–06
Hickman Bridge 91–92

Hidden Canyon Trail 148–51
Hidden Garden Canyon
   157–60
Highway 12 29, 34
hoodoos 38–39, 40, 111, 117, 120,
   124, 126, 128
horseback riding 131, 132, 162

Island in the Sky 71, 74–81
itineraries 23–34

Junior Ranger program 14–15

Landscape Arch 56
Lava Point Campground 164
The Lodge (Bryce Canyon) 133

The Maze 71, 72
Mesa Arch 74–75
Moab 27, 31–32, 33
Monument Valley 27, 33
Mossy Cave 128–30
mountain biking 26, 27, 33, 68
Navajo Loop Trail 124–26
navigation 13
The Narrows 154
The Needles 71, 72
North Campground 134
North Window 64–65

outdoor etiquette 16, 59, 80

Park Avenue 63–64
Peek-a-Boo Loop 131
Petroglyph Walk 90–91
Pine Tree Arch 54–56

Queens Garden 121–23

rafting 32, 33, 42–43, 84
Rim Trail 119–21
Riverside Walk (Temple of
   Sinawava) 152–53
rock climbing 67–68, 82, 161–62

safety 12–13, 41, 171–77
Sand Dune 49–52
South Campground 164
South Window 64–65
stargazing 39–40, 79–80, 81
Sunset Campground 134–35
Sunset Point to Sunrise Point
   117–18

Timber Creek Overlook Trail
   (Kolob Canyon) 160
Tunnel Arch 54–56
Turret Arch 64–65

Upheaval Dome 78

Walhalla Overlook 168–69
Wall Arch 44
Waterpocket Fold 29
weather 20–21, 171–73
Weeping Rock Trail 148
Whale Rock 79–80
wildlife viewing 66–67, 82, 106–07,
   131–32, 160–61
Willow Flat Campground 85

Zion National Park 18, 23–24, 28,
   41–42, 136–64
   campgrounds in 163–64
   getting to 141–43
   hiking in 143–60
   lodges in 163
Zion Lodge (Zion) 163

Credit: Kaden McAllister

ABOUT THE AUTHORS

Harley McAllister works as a project manager but is most alive when he is outdoors, especially with his wife, Abby, and their boys. He has lived in seven different states and on three different coasts, including four years with his family in the Dominican Republic teaching at a nonprofit school. Harley has rafted, skied, snorkeled, backpacked, mountain-biked, and camped in diverse locations in both North and South America. He has spent a lot of time off the pavement and loves to share his passions with others to inspire them to get outside more often, and have fun doing it.

Abby McAllister is a sometimes-harried mom of four boys, an outdoor enthusiast, a kitchen chemist, and copy-cat crafter. Together, she and her husband, Harley, have traveled the world always seeking opportunities to get their boys out exploring nature. When she is not outside, she is busy writing books and blogs that will help other people get their kids unplugged and outside.

Get more travel tips at the McAllisters' website:
www.our4outdoors.com